DISPLAY OF
POWER

HOW FUBU CHANGED A WORLD OF FASHION, BRANDING AND LIFESTYLE

By DAYMOND JOHN
with DANIEL PAISNER

To contact the author, please check out the following:

www.myspace.com/Daymond John
www.stealthbrandingcorp.com
www.mogulsonly.com
www.displayofpower.com

Published in Nashville, Tennessee, by NAKED INK™, a division of the General Trade Book Group of Thomas Nelson Publishers, Inc. Please visit us at www.nakedink.net.

Library of Congress Cataloging-in-Publication data on file with the Library of Congress.

ISBN 10: 1-59555-853-5
ISBN 13: 978-1-59555-853-4

Printed in the United States of America
07 08 09 10 — 5 4 3 2 1

"Have you lost your mind? I mean, how is it that you can disrespect a man's ethnicity when you know we've influenced nearly every facet of white America? From our music to our style of dress, not to mention your basic imitation of our sense of cool. Walk, talk, dress, mannerisms . . . we enrich your very existence, all the while contributing to the gross national product through our achievements in corporate America. It's these conceits that comfort me when I am faced with the ignorant, cowardly, bitter and bigoted, who have no talent, no guts. People like you who desecrate things they don't understand, when the truth is, you should say, 'Thank you, man!' and go on about your way. But apparently you are incapable of doing that! And don't tell me to be cool. I am cool."

—Cedric the Entertainer as "Sin LaSalle"
in *Be Cool*

Dedication

THEY SAY THAT BEHIND EVERY STRONG MAN IS A STRONG WOMAN. WELL, I HAVE FOUR BEHIND ME, AND THAT'S POWER! AND SO I DEDICATE THIS BOOK TO THE FOUR POWERFUL WOMEN IN MY LIFE—BECAUSE TOGETHER, WE'RE UNSTOPPABLE!

>> MARGOT JOHN . . . MY MOTHER . . . FOR GIVING ME LIFE, COURAGE, HONOR, DISCIPLINE, AND FOR PUTTING HER DREAMS ON HOLD FOR ME TO HAVE A FIGHTING CHANCE. FOR BEING BOTH MY MOTHER AND FATHER, AND LEADING ME DOWN THE RIGHT PATH, EVEN IF THAT MEANT LETTING ME GO DOWN THE WRONG PATH TO FIGURE IT OUT FOR MYSELF.

>> MARIA . . . MY EX-WIFE . . . FOR BEING THERE FOR ME FROM THE BEGINNING, AND FOR SHOWING ME WHAT TRUE LOVE IS AND TRYING TO SET ME STRAIGHT WHEN I WAS OUT OF CONTROL. FOR DISAGREEING WITH ME WHEN I HAD TOO MANY YES MEN AROUND. FOR RAISING OUR KIDS WITH A DEDICATION AND FOCUS THAT CAN RARELY BE FOUND IN THE PARENTS OF TODAY. THE ONLY REASON I CAN STAY FOCUSED ON MY WORK IS BECAUSE I NEVER HAVE TO WORRY ABOUT ANYTHING ELSE IN MY WORLD IF YOU HAVE ANYTHING TO DO WITH IT.

>> DESTINY AND YASMEEN . . . MY DAUGHTERS . . . FOR INSPIRING ME EVERY DAY. FOR BEING THE ONLY TWO PEOPLE IN MY LIFE WHO DON'T NEED TO THANK ME FOR ANYTHING, BUT WHO DO ANYWAY. YOU ARE SENT FROM GOD. I TRULY BELIEVE THAT. YOU ARE HUMBLE, TALENTED AND BEAUTIFUL, INSIDE AND OUT. DADDY LOVES YOU.

contents

contents

It was 1997. I'd just started making some money. I was driving a brand new Lexus GS400. Gold. My girlfriend was renting a house in Rockville Centre—a mostly rich, mostly white neighborhood on Long Island. I was feeling pretty good. I stopped for gas on Sunrise Highway, on my way home from the city. It was late, but not too late. There were other people at the gas station, but not too many. I didn't recognize anyone in particular, but someone must have recognized me.

I got back to my girlfriend's house and took the dog out for a walk. A little Chow Chow puppy named Coco. My girlfriend came outside, too, and we were in front of the house just a couple minutes when we noticed a black guy coming down the street, looking a little out of place. He looked a little shady. Grimy. Shifty. Hair all undone. Like he was up to something.

Now, who was I to talk, right? Me, a black man in a white neighborhood, not exactly the George Jefferson type, walking a little puppy, middle of the night. Who can say, maybe I looked a little shady too. But I knew my business, and I'd never seen this other guy before. He passed by once and turned the corner. I thought, This is not good.

My girlfriend didn't like the looks of this guy either, so she hopped in the car to follow him, see what he was up to. I couldn't call the cops, just because someone looked out of place. It had happened to me too many times. Maybe I had no bus fare, so I had to walk, sometimes through a nice neighborhood. Maybe my car broke down, and there was no public transportation. Things happen. I didn't want to jump to conclusions and convict this guy for no good reason.

Well, he must have doubled back and hopped the fence around the house, because the next thing I knew he was walking up to me from behind, asking, "Hey, you got the time?" Right then, I knew what was coming. Right then, I thought I was dead. It took a couple weeks for me to put two and two together and figure that someone I knew must have seen me at that gas station on Sunrise Highway, someone from my old neighborhood, someone who knew I was finally making money, and that my ride was probably insured, and they could 'jack the car and it wouldn't cost me a thing. All of this hit me a little later on, but soon as I heard those words—"Hey, you got the time?"—all I could think was, This guy's gonna kill me. Last time I heard that line I was with my father in Central Park, fishing. I was about eight. Someone sidled up to us and asked my father for the time, and my father started beating the crap out of him. Just like that. I'd thought my father had gone completely crazy, beating down this guy like that. He had a short fuse, my father, but this was over the top, even for him. It wasn't until years later that I realized what had happened. Only other time in my life I'd ever been jumped, or robbed, and this black guy in Rockville Centre uses the same line.

"Hey, you got the time?"

This guy pulled out the biggest gun I'd ever seen, and led me to the backyard. Put the gun to my head, told me to lay face down on the ground. I had a nice gold chain around my neck, and he pulled it off. He told me to empty everything from my pockets. In those days, I carried a wallet with all my credit cards and papers all rolled up and held together with a rubber band, but there was also about $1000 in there. The guy didn't even see the money. He took the loose change in my pocket, and the keys to the car.

I lay there, face down, and realized I'd heard a million of these stories. Some of my boys, they'd been on the dishing-out end of the same scene, and they'd told these stories into the ground. I'd never been on the receiving end, but I knew how it would go. I heard this cat cock his gun. I said, "It's all good, it's all good. You got what you wanted. I'm not calling the cops. Why don't you just take my shoes, so I can't run after you?"

That was the code on the streets, when you wanted to keep someone from chasing after you, you'd take their kicks. It was as good as tying them to a pole.

But he didn't take my shoes. He just drove his knee into my back, pressed the gun against the base of my skull and my face into the cool grass, and in that long moment while I was waiting for what would happen next to actually get around to happening, I could see my life flash before my eyes. Wasn't the only thing I thought about. I also thought about my girlfriend, and hoped like hell she wouldn't come back until this punk had left the scene. (She didn't, thank God.) But mostly I thought about my life. Sounds like a cliché, I know, but it's the God's honest truth. I closed my eyes and saw it all, and I thought, Man, how did I get here?

HOME

I grew up in Hollis, Queens, in a single-family house on Farmers Boulevard. LL Cool J was from Hollis, a couple years ahead of me, and on one of his early raps he talked about Farmers Boulevard. That was like hard cash, to be able to say you lived on the same street LL talked about in one of his songs, and to be able to back it up. "Christmas in Hollis," by Run DMC. Another great song that really put us on the map—on the map, in the air, all around.

More than anything else, it was my neighborhood that defined me. I guess that's true for a lot of people, but in my case it was a neighborhood that was crackling with heat and haste and energy. Things were popping in Hollis. That was where I first got my world view, where I developed the will to succeed, where I formed my first ideas about people, where I first got excited about something beyond cars, cash and clothes. Hell, it's where I learned right from wrong— even if it took me a couple slips to tell the two apart. I didn't need to hear it in a song for it to be a part of me, and I didn't need some advertising copy writer to sell it to me, either. Like I said, it was in the air, and it would form the basis for everything that came next.

I was actually born in Brooklyn, but we moved to Queens back before I can remember, and for a while I ran against the numbers in my neighborhood because I had both parents living with me under the same roof. The single-parent model wasn't so common when I was in grade school, but as I grew up you'd see it more and more. It changed as I got older—and not for the better. Most times, it was just the mom, raising the kids. Sometimes, it was the dad. A lot of times it was a grandparent, or an older relative. After that, it was an intact nuclear family, so we were kind of the exception on our street, by the time I hit my teens. We owned our own house. We were the American ideal that didn't really reflect what was going on.

My mother, Margot John, is African-American. My father, Garfield John, was from Trinidad. He came to this country on his own when he was a teenager. That tells you something about him, I guess. My father was motivated and adventurous and not afraid to go out and stake his claim. You could say the same things about me. I got my start in business because I stuck my neck out, and so did my father when he was a young man. We're completely different people, but in this way we were cut the same. He ended up renting a room in my mother's parents' home. That's how they met, and by the time I was born he was a computer programmer. That was his main thing. All those little manila computer cards they used to have, back in the 1970s, back when computers were these giant, slow-moving machines, they used to be strewn all over the place when I was a little kid. All these dots and codes, like it was some secret language only my father could understand.

By the time I was nine or ten, though, the numbers kind of caught up to us, because my father moved out of the house and my mother filed for divorce. I went from aberration to statistic—or, at least, I stepped into line with the statistics. I became like everyone else in my neighborhood. At some point I looked up and realized that every-thing about my father was just dots and codes. He was feeding me a bunch of crap, and feeding my mother a bunch of crap. One lie after another. One excuse after another. It got to where I told him I never wanted to see him again, never wanted to speak to him, and that's how we left it. At about twelve years old, I was done with him. I was done, and he was gone, and you'll notice that I write about him here in the past tense. He's dead to me, gone, and I'm clear on that. Far as I know, he's alive and well and messing with someone else's head, but he's out of mine.

Yeah, I was only twelve, but I was old enough to realize he was lying to me and my mother, and old enough to stand up to it. I refused to be his puppet. I told him on the phone one day to never, ever call me again, and he knew I was serious. That was the last time we spoke. Even at twelve, I was a decisive, hard-headed person, enough to write off one-half of my support system, to cut myself off from my entire extended family on my father's side. He told them all to never speak to me again. Twenty people I was close to—aunts, uncles, cousins, grandparents—gone with that one move. And I'm still that way, although I'll admit there have been times when that decisiveness has cost me, as I will make clear over these pages. I'll even admit that it might have cost me my relationship with my father and his family, because he was into some things I might have understood a little bit better from an adult perspective. The kind of things that if they came up now, knowing what I know, I might cut him some slack. That's one of the great lessons I took from my father into my own role as a parent: Don't lie to your kids, because they'll grow up and figure you out.

It wasn't a whole lot different, him being around or him not being around. Life was pretty much the same, either way. My father was a typical West Indian dad, which basically meant he wasn't there a whole lot. He was always working. Maybe we went fishing on one of his rare days off, usually out at Oak Beach, on Long Island, but we didn't speak all that much. I was an only child, so it's not like there were any other kids competing for his attention, but the only time he really talked to me was to discipline me, or correct my homework. That was the extent of our relationship. And usually, the way he disciplined me, he'd get out the belt. That's the way he grew up, back in Trinidad. The older I got, the more I started to get into this or that, the more he'd threaten me, and then my mother would get in between us and he'd just go off and smoke a cigarette. He wasn't abusive, wasn't doing anything different than any of the other fathers in my neighborhood, but that's how it was. In Trinidad, in Hollis, Queens . . . it was basically the same.

He was a short man, my father, about five foot six, and I figured out later he must have had a Napoleonic complex. I read up on it and it made sense. He looked like this singer SuperCat, only shorter. To this day, I can't listen to SuperCat or look at one of his videos without thinking of my father. He was always mad about something. He had that short temper, left me thinking about that time in Central Park, when he jumped that guy who was about to rob us, when I thought he was completely crazy. He would even go into a store with a big old "No Smoking" sign pasted up on the wall, and blow smoke in the security guard's face, like he was challenging him to do something about it. He could be real arrogant. That was one of his things, and it would always make me cringe. He was a chronic smoker, so I never smoked. Every time someone would light up it reminded me of him, so I turned away from it. It was the flip side of how I followed my mother, and not my father, how he became a positive influence in the negative. I did just the opposite of whatever he was doing and figured I'd come out okay.

Don't get me wrong, I'm very proud of my Trinidian heritage. It's who I am. That whole West Indian thing, it was a big part of my life when I was a kid, a big part of our family dynamic. It wasn't just the discipline at home, or the cool, distant father stuff. It was the whole male-female relationship, a unique way of looking at the world. With

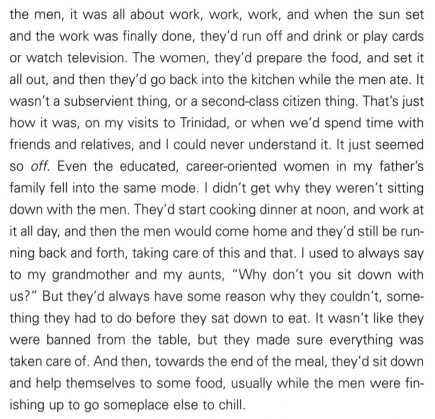

the men, it was all about work, work, work, and when the sun set and the work was finally done, they'd run off and drink or play cards or watch television. The women, they'd prepare the food, and set it all out, and then they'd go back into the kitchen while the men ate. It wasn't a subservient thing, or a second-class citizen thing. That's just how it was, on my visits to Trinidad, or when we'd spend time with friends and relatives, and I could never understand it. It just seemed so *off*. Even the educated, career-oriented women in my father's family fell into the same mode. I didn't get why they weren't sitting down with the men. They'd start cooking dinner at noon, and work at it all day, and then the men would come home and they'd still be running back and forth, taking care of this and that. I used to always say to my grandmother and my aunts, "Why don't you sit down with us?" But they'd always have some reason why they couldn't, something they had to do before they sat down to eat. It wasn't like they were banned from the table, but they made sure everything was taken care of. And then, towards the end of the meal, they'd sit down and help themselves to some food, usually while the men were finishing up to go someplace else to chill.

I used to think maybe they felt out of place, my aunts and my female cousins. Or maybe it was just how they were cut, what they were used to. It wasn't until I was older that I realized they liked it this way. It was what they knew, how they were. I looked closer and saw there was real joy in the work, in preparing food for their families, in taking care of their men, and they seemed to relish in it together. It was simple and pure—something closer to the Italian model than, say, to the Japanese. A real island thing.

My mother never bought into that. She would fall into the same pattern when we were with my father's family, but when it was just the three of us, at home, she had a whole different attitude. She was a really, really strong woman. Still is. Hands down, she was the most important person in my life while I was growing up, the dominant influence, and it's a good thing, too. She was willful, independent, resourceful, driven. All those good things—and, hopefully, some of them rubbed off on me. She told you what was on her mind, what she thought you needed to know. And the great kicker is she's a beautiful woman. Sometimes she looks dead-on like Donna Summer. Sometimes she looks like Diana Ross. She hates it when people compare her to Donna Summer.

My mother's background was completely different than my father's. She grew up in Brooklyn, on the same block as Earl Graves, the founder and publisher of *Black Enterprise* magazine, and Frankie Crocker, a pioneer of R&B radio at WBLS-FM in New York, and a whole bunch of people who turned out to be extremely successful and accomplished, so she was surrounded by aspiring, dedicated people, even as a young girl. She went to Boys and Girls High. She competed in the first Miss Black America contest, and in one of the preliminary Miss America pageants, to represent the state of New York. She was into jazz and dance. She was one of the first black females to work in the Playboy club in New York, as a hostess, but she wanted better than that. She wanted more. She was a real striving, enterprising soul. She used to keep one of those giant two-foot can openers hanging on the wall in our house, with the words "Think Big" printed across it, and that was like her mantra. She used to say, "It takes the same energy to think small as to think big." Whenever I went to her, thinking one way about something, she'd say, "Bigger." Whatever I wanted out of life, she'd say, "Bigger." I grew up wanting a little bit more. I was taught to aim high.

>> MOTHER KNOWS BEST

I get my discipline, my focus, and my drive from my mother. Like a lot of my boys from the neighborhood, that's were It begins and ends for me. You have to realize, she was never the kind of mother who studied all these parenting guides, or did things by the book, but she had a way about her. She knew her stuff, and what she didn't know she managed to figure out.

One of the biggest things she did, back when I was about to start high school, was take out a mortgage on the house so she could stop working. Eighty-thousand dollars, which she figured would be enough for us to live on for three or four years, long enough to help steer me through the period of time she thought I'd be most vulnerable to the negative influences of our neighborhood. She'd always worked two or three jobs, but she wanted to be a little more present in my life just then, to make sure I didn't go down the wrong path. And she was. She didn't hover over me, but she was always around. Like a stealth watchdog. I didn't always notice her, but she was there. And she made me a promise. She knew that clothes were impor- tant to me, that my appearance was important to me, so she told me that if I kept up my grades in school she'd do whatever she had to do to keep decent clothes on my back, so I could have my self- respect. The two went hand-in-hand, far as I was concerned. We didn't have a lot of money, but she said, "Daymond, I don't care what it takes. I'll sell my body if I have to. You just worry about your end."

She could be so outrageous, so raunchy, but I

got her point. That's how she was. First time I went away to summer camp, she gave me a bunch of condoms. I was only twelve, and she's loading me up with condoms because she's trying to be a realist and because she knew what kids were in to. I don't think it ever occurred to her that I'd wind up selling them to the other kids at camp, but that wasn't the point. She was just on top of it, you know. Nothing she got out of any book, or picked up on any talk show, because what mother in her right mind talks to her teenage son about selling her body? Or gives him condoms before he heads off to summer camp? But my mother told it straight. And she backed it up. I always had some decent pants, decent shirts, decent kicks until I scraped together enough money on my own to buy these things for myself. And she watchdogged me. She had my back.

When I was a little older, and my friends started drinking or taking drugs, she told me to bring some of it home and she'd do it with me, right at our kitchen table. She'd never taken any drugs, but she said, "If you want to experiment, we'll experiment together." I thought, How sick is that? Turned me off to the whole deal, but she knew what she was doing. She put me in her shoes—and herself in mine. She knew the idea of me getting high with her was probably the ultimate buzz kill, and she was dead on. I still went out and did stuff with my friends, but nothing heavy, maybe because I couldn't get that image out of my head, of my mother doing the same thing.

Like I said, she was on the low about this stuff. Subtle. For a stretch in there, she used to keep a jigsaw puzzle going. Seems like nothing now, but those jigsaw puzzles were a huge thing with us. Every couple months, we'd get started on a new one. I'd come home from school, I'd sit down, we'd work on the puzzle, and we'd get to talking. I didn't even realize it, but she would draw stuff out of me. It was a great little trick of hers. We'd work the puzzle, and I'd have no idea she was pumping me for information, or that I was really listening to whatever it was she had to say. And she'd pass on these pearls of wisdom—like, you don't get rich off your day job, you get rich off your homework—and I'd soak it up. I read the same thing in a book, a couple years later, but back then I had no idea what she was talking about.

Of course, on some level, I guess I knew full well. I knew my mother was always working those two or three jobs, and she still came home and went to work on something else. She started making clothes. She tried to get a car service going. She tried to get a catering deal going. And I came to realize that whatever job she did out of the house, she was working for someone else. She would always hit a glass ceiling. But this other stuff, this getting-rich-off-your-homework-business, there was no limit to what she could accomplish. And the truth is, nothing ever came of any of that, but that didn't stop her. She kept at it. She sold some of her clothes, but it never amounted to much, and still she'd tell me it was fulfilling. She'd get something out of it. She'd tell me, "Sometimes it's doing what you love that makes you rich. Sometimes, it's having something to dream about."

Here's another thing you need to know about my mother, because it plays into what happened next. She was a talented seamstress. It could have been a career for her, if she didn't have all these other things going on. She sewed a lot of my clothes, in part because money was tight but also because she really enjoyed making me nice things and knowing I appreciated them. When I was old enough she taught me how to work a sewing machine and put me to work finishing some of her pieces. Before long, I could sew a button or hem a pant leg. My mother prided herself on the fact that her clothes didn't look cheap or homemade. A lot of kids, their mothers would make them something and it'd look like crap. But my mother's clothes were hot.

Let me get back to that *aim high* business for a minute. Like most kids in my neighborhood, it took a while for my aim to catch up with my mother's expectations. I missed the mark from time to time. Hell, I missed the mark *most* of the time. I ran every kind of hustle, even in first or second grade. The older I got, the more I bent the rules. My big racket in grade school was selling pencils. I'd pick up all the dropped pencils I could find in school, or pinch loose pencils when their owners weren't looking, then I'd shave the yellow paint off the sides with a pen knife so they were no longer identifiable, put my own little designs on them and sell them for a quarter. I'd collect all the other kids' lunch money, selling them their own pencils, which I guess put me somewhere between a budding entrepreneur and a budding hustler.

One of my other hustles, early on, was to tramp through the dumpster behind the glass factory, around the block from my house. They used to throw out all these slightly damaged mirrors, all these irregular pieces, and I'd collect what seemed salvageable and smooth out the rough edges with sandpaper and sell them for a dollar or so, as compacts. The girls would just grab this stuff up. I'd work the street corners by my house, or take them to school. And I wasn't the only one doing it. There were a bunch of us in that dumpster, only the other guys would just collect the glass and smash it someplace else, or throw it at girls. Best I can remember, I was the only one who thought to sell it to the girls, to turn them into customers, so I guess you could say my entrepreneurial streak wasn't shared with the other kids in my neighborhood. I saw opportunity, where everyone else saw distraction. I made a market, where they were just making noise.

I was always doing something to make money, because in my neighborhood money was power. It kept us going. I'm not talking about keeping our household going, or buying groceries, but the money you had in your pocket. The "I Got Bank" money. That was the measure of the man you might become. It was an all-important gauge, how you valued yourself, how others looked back at you.

When I was about ten, I started picking up these used bikes people would leave out on the street for the trash collector. I would take the parts that were still good and stockpile them and after a while I started building some good, working bikes out of other people's garbage. Sometimes I'd get used parts from the local bike store, on Jamaica Avenue. I'd go in there with my mother's boyfriend Steve, who turned up when I was about twelve and quickly became like a father to me. He took an interest in what I was doing, and he tried to help me out.

I turned my backyard into a little factory. I was always out patrolling the neighborhood, looking for a certain-size tire, or a decent seat, or a reasonable-enough looking set of handlebars. There was another kid named Tony, he was a couple years younger than me, and I put him to work as my assistant. We were forever in search of parts. I don't know that I paid Tony all that much, but I must have given him something, maybe a bike every once in a while. Something to keep him committed to the enterprise. Probably as little as I could get away with, instead of as much as I could afford. He ended up driving for me a bunch of years later, after I'd gotten FUBU off the ground, and working as my assistant, so I must have been a decent boss when I was a kid, else he would never have come back for more.

'Course, I didn't credit my mother at the time, but I took her words to heart. Her line about how you get rich off your homework made a whole lot of sense to me, and from that point on I had a sideline going. I kept thinking big. And I made sure there was always something to dream about.

>> DRIVE (LITERALLY)

My mother was always trying to get something off the ground, to turn some sideline into a frontline business. For a year or two, she worked this livery route at night, in and around Hollis. It was a real West Indian move. A lot of people we knew from the islands were into the same thing, so she decided to go for it. All you needed was a car, and a customer with someplace else to be. Nobody worried about cab licenses or city regulations or anything like that.

When I was older, I ran a van route of my own, in South Jamaica, and I got the idea from my mom. Going back to when I was a kid, I'd sit with her in the front of our Eldorado, our family car, at the butt end of rush hour, picking up the commuters as they came out of the subway station at 179th Street and Hillside Avenue, and for 50 cents they'd jump in the car and we'd car-pool them home, straight along the Q2 bus route in Hollis.

We weren't licensed. We weren't catching fares for an established company. We were just there, looking for people who needed a ride home after work, people who didn't want to bother with the bus. It was a tough way to earn some extra money, and it wasn't the best environment for me—it was actually dangerous, running all over town on a school night—but we'd ferry these strangers home and in-between the pick-ups and the drop-offs my mother would teach me about people. She'd say, "Daymond, did you notice the way that last customer said thank you when we dropped him off?" Or, "That one will be successful, 'cause he looks you in the eye." Whatever it was, she'd see it as some teaching opportunity, and we'd drive on through the night—me doing my homework, my mother schooling me between carloads, the money coming in a dollar at a time, keeping us ahead of our bills.

There was one hustle after another, and most of them were on the straight side of legit, and pretty soon I started looking for paying jobs wherever I could find them. I'd hand out fliers announcing the opening of the Jamaica Coliseum, or I'd roam the booths at the flea market on Rockaway Boulevard and be an extra set of eyes and ears for all these vendors. I don't think I was ever without a job, from the time I was ten years old, and on top of each job was a hustle. This flea market "security" gig was a little strange. I'd tell the vendors when people were stealing, and they'd throw me five dollars for my trouble. I realized early on that if I put together enough clients, I could really maximize my profits, because as long as I was on the scene and on the clock patrolling one booth, I might as well patrol the booths nearby at the same time. So I set about convincing as many vendors as I could that they needed my services.

Trouble was, this one gig didn't last all that long, because I didn't see myself as a snitch, although if I was a little more conniving and scheming I might have seen an opportunity playing both sides, collecting money from the vendors to guard their booths and another chunk of change from my boys for looking the other way while they lifted some goods. That would have been the way to play it, but that wasn't me, at least not just yet, even though it does give you an idea of the mindset you develop in a neighborhood like Hollis. *Get rich or die tryin'*—that could have been our credo all the way back then, and as we got older our hustles got a little less innocent, a little more involved, a little more suspect. I started to make my share of trouble, and to run with a crowd that made even more. That's just how it was, and I don't set that out to justify my behavior but to set the scene. Where I come from, you got caught up in the same currents that moved everyone else, or you got left behind. We used to say we'd either be dead or in jail by the time we hit twenty, so we didn't think that far out. Everything was all about the moment. There was no planning for any future, because you couldn't count on any future.

After a while, I started to realize that the money I could make on my nickel-and-dime enterprises would never amount to the paper I needed to get the things I wanted or the respect on the street I was starting to crave, so I looked to a bunch of minimum wage-type jobs. I worked at a cookie store. I worked at a popcorn stand. I worked the deep fryer at Church's Fried Chicken, which was probably the nastiest job you could have. Back then, minimum wage was about $4.00 an hour, and maybe they paid as much as $5.00 at some of these places, but it was just pure drudgery, you know. A slow train to no place you wanted to be. The trick was hanging around long enough to figure out a way to beat whatever system they had you working, before management figured out you were on to something and got around to firing you. And then all you did was bounce to some other job, around some other corner. That's the great tug-and-pull of these low-paying jobs, in our poorest communities, and I got caught up in it for a while: lose one job and there's always another to take its place, and still no clear way to get ahead.

First time I saw any kind of real money was when I took a job as a junior counselor at a Y camp in upstate New York, in a town called Tuxedo. Tall Timbers, that was the name of the place. Wasn't exactly *honest* money, but it was real enough. The deal was, most summers, I would go away for a month or two at a time to visit family or friends—in California, Hawaii, Bermuda, Canada, Trinidad—wherever my mom could arrange for a place for me to stay. It's like she had her own little Fresh Air Fund program going. Her idea was to get me out of the city, but she also wanted me to see that there were other ways of life out there, other points of view I might take up as my own. Plus, she wanted me to see the world. Already, she could see I might wind up running with a questionable crowd, and she probably thought that if she exposed me to enough positive influences I might make some better choices. It wasn't a bad strategy, because I really did take to some of these places. Pace of life, priorities, practical concerns . . . everything was a little different outside of Hollis, and my mother was smart to open that up to me.

And then she sent me to this YMCA camp one summer, when I was about twelve years old, and I liked it enough to re-up as a junior counselor when I was fourteen. You had to be a certain age before they felt you were mature enough to be in a position of responsibility, but I don't think they figured on me and my boys Carl and Omar. Oh, we were mature and responsible, alright, but you couldn't really count on us to stay within the bounds of civil behavior. We probably bent every rule they had at that camp, and a couple local laws besides. But that was just after-hours stuff. When I was actually working, they had me taking care of handicapped kids, which I thought was pretty cool. It was a general camp, with a general population, but they did have a small group of kids who were emotionally or physically disabled, and that's where I was assigned. I liked it well enough. We all got along. There'd be one or two kids I was assigned to personally, and then I also had some general responsibilities. And for the most part I was a model counselor, but there was a whole lot of wiggle room in *the most part*. Anyway, far as any of the camp directors knew, I was a model counselor. Put a camera on me, though, and you wouldn't have to look through too much tape to find evidence to the contrary.

The pay was next to nothing, and we couldn't count on any kind of meaningful tip money, so it was inevitable that a bunch of teenage counselors would come up with at least a couple ways to up their take-home. The summer was broken down into four or five different sessions. Every two weeks, one group of campers would leave and a new group would come in. It only took a session for me to figure the place out. After that, I had that camp wired. I got pretty good at the bumper pool table they had in the rec hall, and I turned myself into a real pool shark by the end of the summer, hustling all the other counselors and campers out of their pocket money. After a while, I started going into town on my evenings off, loading up on cigarettes and beer, and then coming back to camp and selling the stuff at a premium. Campers, counselors . . . I'd sell to anybody, with a real nice mark-up for my trouble. I'd also brought a couple bags of weed with me, up from New York, and I sold off my stash, one joint at a time. I didn't think of it as dealing. I thought of it as sharing—and it just worked out these the people I was sharing with were sharing their money with me in return. That was my take on it.

It wasn't exactly my shining hour. We had a scam going where we'd steal all kinds of stuff from the campers, and then sell it to the next group of campers in for the next session. We'd never steal from the handicapped kids in my care, that's where I drew my moral lines, but everyone else was fair game. All the other kids in the camp's general population, we'd grab their flashlights, their batteries, their hand-held video games, whatever they'd leave lying around. Anything we thought we could re-sell. Our business plan was, if they weren't smart enough to lock up their stuff and keep it from their grimy counselors, it deserved to be stolen. It was on them.

Our biggest haul was flashlights. One session, we must have grabbed about fifty. Some high-end lanterns, some crappy little Eveready plastic numbers. We tied them up in plastic bags we'd borrowed from the kitchen, to keep them dry, and hid them under a huge boulder in the woods. And it's not like it went unnoticed, all these flashlights gone missing. The camp used to hold these gatherings at night, and everyone would sit around the fire, but nobody had any flashlights because we had taken them all. Nobody could get back and forth to the campfire without bumping into someone else.

It became such a problem that the camp director got up and started screaming one night, because nobody could see a thing. The veins were popping on his neck, that's how mad he was. He couldn't understand what had happened to all the flashlights. He knew something was up, but he didn't have anything on any of us. So he just screamed out to the whole camp one night, "What the hell is going on? Is somebody trying to open up a disco?" He looked so confused, so helpless. *Beaten.* We just thought that was the funniest thing we'd ever seen—only we couldn't laugh too hard without giving ourselves away.

We were like a rustic chop shop or trading post, fencing all these camping goods and making good money. And it piled up quick. I remember coming home to Queens at the end of that summer with about two thousand dollars, between my salary and tips, my bumper pool winnings, and my second-hand trading post operation. I was only supposed to earn a couple hundred bucks, and here I came back with all this money. I was fourteen years old, and it was all the money in the world. I ended up buying my first car almost as soon as I came home—a 1969 Mustang, white, a little beat up but still running. My mother had promised to match whatever money I took home from summer camp. So she ended up kicking in a couple grand. We used to say Ford could stand for two things, depending on what you could afford; I didn't have the money to buy the Ford that stood for First On Race Day; my Ford stood for Found On Road Dead.

My mother was cool. She must have known what was going on; in fact, I'm certain she did. She knew what it cost, a car like that. Even a "hoopty" costs money, and she knew what I was supposed to be making in salary that summer. I told her I did really well in tips, but she didn't buy it. Even so, she left me alone. That's how she usually played it, when I got into stuff like that. She kept her eye on me, but she let it slide, like she was waiting for me to figure things out for myself. And I usually did, eventually. It's just that it took a big chunk of time for *eventually* to roll around, and in the meantime we didn't have money for a car like that—especially for a car I couldn't even drive.

But that was my mother's great strength, her wisdom: she gave me a little rope, thinking I would either hang myself with it, or use it to lift myself up and out.

>> WHO MOVED MY GOVERNMENT CHEESE?

It's one thing to be poor. It's another thing to be without pride or self-respect, and my mother saw to it that our pockets were never empty in this department. We held our heads up. She taught me that being poor was a state of mind, and I grew up thinking we were rich even though we didn't have any money. We were rich in what mattered. She kept me in those decent clothes. We lived in our own house—free and clear, until my mother took out that money so she could spend more time at home with me. We never went hungry. But money was always tight. We weren't digging in garbage cans or anything like that, but some months we worried if we'd have enough for the electric bill. We were always scraping.

The house on Farmers Boulevard, that was our nut. My mother used to say that real estate was the most important thing you could own. It was right there in the name. "Real estate." Something you could build on. Something real.

All that scraping, early on, got me thinking. I used to pick up these giant blocks of government cheddar from my friend Carl Brown, who's now one of my FUBU partners. I'd known Carl since we were six years old. His grandfather was a minister, and his parents would become ministers, and we used to get a lot of that subsidized food and supplies from them. Powdered milk. Eggs. Pasta. When my mother was working her crazy schedule, she'd leave the food out for me to cook for myself. She taught me how to get around the kitchen.

At eight, I could make a mean plate of spaghetti, or a mess of scrambled eggs, and when I started to move around town on my own, in and out of the bodegas and mom-and-pop stores that lined the streets of Hollis and Jamaica, I started to realize how much everything cost. I'd hear it from my mother, too. She'd drive to the white neighborhoods, because our money went a little further there. I'd think, It doesn't make sense how all these goods are more expensive in the ghetto. Groceries. Hardware. Household items. And we were buying a much lower cut of meat, for example. That was the first time in my life I realized how tough it is on our poorer classes. It's like everything's conspiring against you, even the basic cost of living.

And so you adapt. You recognize that the deck is stacked against you, but you play it anyway. You work a little harder, save a little more aggressively, plan a little more diligently. You drive a bit out of your way, to shop in the white neighborhoods. You find a reason to go to the butcher on the Upper West Side, to get that better cut of meat for your family. You buy in bulk. You take those food stamps, if you're entitled to them, and you use them with your head held high. You reach out to your friends for that block of government cheese. Whatever you have to do to get and keep an edge, that's what you do, and at the same time you continue to support the small store owners in your community, because they rely on your dollars every bit as much as you rely on them to maintain that sense of community that you've come to value.

So there we were, with a car I couldn't drive—a car I couldn't *afford*—and soon enough we had spent down the $80,000 mortgage on the house. It's not like we blew the money. We lived off of it, for nearly three years. My mother used it to buy herself some time away from work, to keep me out of trouble. We'd been broke before, and now we were broke all over again. A couple times, it looked like the bank might actually foreclose on us, but we got it together and kept ourselves afloat. They'd cut our electricity every now and then, and I remember for a while we had to heat our bathwater on the stove. Sometimes, I'd stand at the stove and give myself a straight-up sponge bath. We lived off food stamps. Every month, it seemed, we'd stand in line at the Con Ed office in Jamaica, and ask for some kind of relief on our electric bill. I look back on those bills now and quietly seethe, because they ran to $600, $700, $800 a month, and years later, after I was finally making real money and living in a big house in a nice part of Long Island, my bills never got close to that. Just another example of how tough it is to get it going when you don't have a whole lot going on.

We were a good team, me and my mother. I look back now and think it's amazing, what I took in, what I learned by example. She sewed, so I learned to sew. She loved to travel, so I learned to love to travel. She worked, more than one job at a time, and she usually worked her own deal on the side, so I learned to work, more than one job at a time, with another side deal always cooking. She mortgaged the house to help pay for something she couldn't provide on her own, and years later, when that mortgage was paid off and I was getting my business going, I did the same thing. It took writing this book and looking back over my shoulder for me to really recognize how much I patterned myself after my mother, and the great, lasting lesson, which I carry with me now as a parent, is that your kids are watching. Always. Whatever you do, they're taking notes, so you better do it well, and get it right, or they'll repeat the same mistakes somewhere further down the road.

That's how it was, with me and my mother. Whatever came our way, we faced it down. We dealt with it. I got through my high school years, through that time she thought I might be headed for trouble, and she went back to work. She got a job with American Airlines, which was a nice bonus because it meant we could fly stand-by anywhere on American's route. Me, I started bouncing from one minimum wage job to the next, and once I started working I tried to be less of a drain on my mother's pocketbook. I don't think I actually contributed to our household expenses, but I took care of my own needs. I bought my own clothes. And a funny thing happened: the older I got, the more I started to strike out on my own, the more it became important to me to be respected in any room I entered. Don't know where that came from, but that was key. Maybe it had to do with my dad, and that Napoleon complex. Maybe it was me overcompensating for how hard we had it, in terms of money. Again, I don't mean to cry poor. We had it better than most. We had our own roof over our heads. But sometimes that roof leaked. Sometimes we couldn't afford to make repairs. And sometimes we had to do without in order to keep what we had.

I met another of my future partners, J Alexander, when I was going to middle school. I'd gone to Catholic school all the way through seventh grade, St. Gerard Magellan in Hollis, but seventh grade didn't really count. Not the first time, anyway. Here's what happened. When my parents were going through their divorce, I started acting up. A lot. School had always been easy to me, but I was failing this, and failing that, and not really caring. The school guidance counselor could see what was going on, and they would have passed me anyway, but my mother did a very unusual and courageous thing. She stepped in and insisted that the school hold me accountable for my actions. I didn't know this at the time, of course. All I knew was that my guidance counselor gave me one last chance to pass one last test. I took the test and failed it on purpose. I didn't get what was at stake, or maybe I did and failed it anyway. And then my mother came in and told the school to fail me, and to make me repeat seventh grade, which was what I deserved. She wanted me to be accountable for my actions, and to know that my parents couldn't bail me out of every situation. And then she told me she was tired of working night and day to send me to private school, if this was how I showed my appreciation. She said she could work two jobs instead of three.

(Just a side note: my mother got skipped twice; my father got skipped once; so I leveled the playing field a little by getting left back.)

Sad to say, my mother wound up taking on that third job again the following summer, just to keep me under lock and key. I'd done something to piss her off and earn myself a summer-long punishment, but she couldn't stay at home from her main job to keep an eye on me so she had to hire some neighborhood lady to watchdog me. And she couldn't afford it, either, so she took another job just to pay the babysitter. Gives you an idea how important discipline was to my mother. Gives you an idea of the lengths she would go to keep me in line. And it gives you an idea how she would stick to her word, no matter what.

Anyway, that's how I ended up in public school, repeating seventh grade, just to prove a point. I went to IS 238, on Hillside Avenue and 182nd Street. It wasn't too far from our house, but it was way out of my comfort zone. These kids were just like monsters to me. It's like they were eating their young. I dreaded going there at first. There was a pretty famous gang, based in the Bronx, but it reached down all the way into that school. Zulu Nation. Those guys were actually at the forefront of the development of rap and hip-hop music in New York City, so this was heavy duty stuff, and to a kid from Catholic school it was night and day. There were fights all the time, and people getting jumped for their sneakers. It was like being sent to prison, that's how I looked at it, like every day you'd half-expect to see camera crews from the six o'clock news.

And then I met J, and we started to hang out. He wasn't like any of my other friends. Walking around in nice, clean, styling clothes wasn't important to him, the way it was important to me. His parents were very restrictive, while my mother was pretty relaxed about a lot of things. He was a real quiet student. I used to catch all kinds of drama from the cool kids for hanging out with him, because it's all about reputation when you're in school, but I didn't listen to any of that. I liked J. Didn't matter to me what my other friends thought about it, and I looked up one day and realized I'd put together my own little rag tag collection of friends, from this and that crowd. I had my "gangsta" friends, my drug dealer friends, my friends who were into music, my friends who were into a little bit of everything. And then I had my friends like J, who kind of did things their own way, and at some point I figured out that it takes all kinds of people to make this world pulse. This world, this neighborhood, whatever . . . Queens basically *was* my whole world at that stage, so even when I was following my mother's advice and thinking big, I wasn't thinking beyond the borough. That was big enough for me.

I've met a lot of successful businessmen and women, and if I had to pick one common trait that links most all of them it's their ability to interact with people. All kinds of people. And that's been the case with me. I've been plugged in to all these different groups, all these different social circles, since way back. And it wasn't a conscious effort on my part. It just worked out that way. I liked what each of these groups, each of these individuals, had to offer, and I was comfortable enough with myself to ease right in to almost any social situation.

Middle school rolled into high school, this time in Bayside. That's where I met Keith Perrin, who also ended up being one of my partners. First time I ever met him, he had a ski cap on, middle of summer. Nowadays, of course, that ski cap is a staple but back then nobody was wearing them in the heat of summer. Didn't matter to Keith, though. He'd just had some kind of accident, and he had this bloody bandage on his head, so he threw the ski cap on to cover it up and went about his day. For some reason, we just hit it off, and as I started to put together this eclectic group of friends, with all these different interests, all these mindsets, I started to feel more and more comfortable in my own skin. I started to put myself out there a little bit, in ways I would have never considered if it had been just me.

LL Cool J and Run DMC and all those guys were just hitting big, and most of them were from Hollis, so music was a big, big thing to us, and we started to see all this money rolling into the neighborhood. Guys riding around in Mercedes Benzes and Alfa Romeos and Jettas and Maximas. Guys flashing some serious jewelry. The money was coming from rap music, and from drugs, and those two rivers of cash flow ran into each other and trickled down to the rest of us. And the thing is, these guys continued to live in the neighborhood, LL and them. Part of that was because rap wasn't paying a whole lot in those days, and even though they'd hit it big, in terms of national exposure and record deals and all that, it didn't necessarily translate into big bucks, and part of that was because Hollis was who they were. I mean, where else were they gonna go?

I knew these guys a little bit. I knew their families. I knew their stories. We all knew each other to say hello, and for a while I took up break dancing and got pretty good at it, so these guys started to know me from that as well. In fact, I spent so much time at it I was offered a spot as a dancer with a group called Houdini, which was popular at the time. They wanted me to go on one of their tours, and I didn't even have the guts to ask my mother if I could. I knew she'd say no, so I just let the offer slide. Turned out they gave my spot to another kid named Jermaine Dupri, who's now a huge player in the music industry. He ended up being the juggernaut of the Atlanta music movement, discovering Kris Kross, Bow Wow, Da Brat and many other artists. Even today, he's one of the most influential people in the music industry, and one of the few people of his stature who's honest and real. He took that Houdini gig and made some real noise with it. I guess he didn't have to ask *his* mother for permission.

>> RE-MIX

Music was a tremendously big deal to me as a kid. It wasn't just the soundtrack to every thing, and it wasn't just me. It had an impact on my whole community. You have to realize, rap music, hip-hop culture, break-dancing . . . it was all tied together, and it was all incredibly exciting and raw and new. It was in our face, you know. These guys were our Beatles, and we were thick in the middle of this incredible new phenomenon, like Hollis was our own little Liverpool. And you could feel it, all around. The music was in the way we moved, the way we talked, the way we dressed. As KRS-1 says, "Hip-hop is not something you do, it's something you live."

For the first time, we started to care about what we put out, how we presented ourselves. There wasn't a FUBU for us to latch onto in those days, so we borrowed from all these different brands and developed our own look, our own style. Adidas, Le Coq Sportif, Izod, Le Tigre, Levi's, Reebok, Lee's . . . this stuff wasn't meant for us, necessarily, but we wore it like it mattered. And it did.

And we knew what we were into. We knew what we liked. We knew this music was important, that it would make a dent, and thirty years later, we're still listening to it. You can make the case that it's the dominant form of music these days, and hip-hop culture has been the driving force behind our success at FUBU, and behind the success of many other brands. But back then, it was all starting to percolate. Back then, we were all starting out. And we all felt like a part of it. It was ours. It started up in the Bronx, but it quickly filtered down to us. Now it's for everybody all across the country—all around the world, even—but at that time it was just for the kids in the inner boroughs of New York City. We owned it.

Very quickly, music became such a central part of our lives that we started following our favorite artists around the country, watching them perform. First part of my life, the music on the radio wasn't really speaking to me. Hall & Oates? The Bee Gees? Not exactly my thing. But things started to change, around the time I hit middle school. All of a sudden, music became our cultural driving force and I got caught up in it, same as everyone else I knew. I was fourteen, fifteen, sixteen years old, and rap promoters were staging these great shows. Artists like the Fat Boys, Run DMC, LL Cool J, Houdini, Public Enemy, Eric B and Rakim, Big Daddy Kane, Slick Rick . . . all on one bill. First one I remember was the Fresh Fest tour, and it was probably the first big rap and hip-hop tour in the country, and we wanted to be a part of it. It was like those old rock 'n roll shows, all these artists taking turns, selling out Madison Square Garden, or these great outdoor stadiums. There were girls and drugs, and money changing hands. It worked out great for me, because I had those flying privileges at American Airlines, so I could jump to this or that city without spending anything, or sometimes we'd take my Mustang, or someone else's van.

And because we knew a lot of the artists, and lived in the same neighborhood, a lot of times they'd throw us a hotel room, and we'd squeeze fifteen people into that room if we had to, just to stretch our money as far as it would go. Or maybe we'd sleep in the van, if money was tight. After a while, there were two or three tours, criss-crossing the country, so there was always a show, somewhere. There was the Bobby Brown tour. There was the New Edition tour. The Fresh Fest became an annual event. So that went on all through high school for me, that's what my weekends were like, chasing these tours up and down the east coast. We lived for them, really.

Before long, a couple of my buddies started working as roadies. Whatever work they could find, to keep close to the action. Some of them dropped out of school. And some of them took their diplomas and figured they'd make it on the back of this rap music phenomenon, which was really just starting to happen in a big way. Hype Williams, the ground-breaking music video director, was from Hollis, as was Irv Gotti, who'd go on to his own ground-breaking (and controversial) career as a record industry mogul. They were both about the same year as me in school, and they were part of this scene too. And the great side benefit to this, of course, was that now we had real access to these artists. Now we could figure out where Big Daddy Kane was staying, and we could follow him down to the Radisson or wherever, and there'd be three hundred girls outside, and we could pass ourselves off as friends of the artists and have these girls crawling all over us, thinking we were the next best thing to being with Big Daddy Kane.

It got to be a game, for those of us on the outside of the inner circle. We'd try to get Big Daddy Kane to shout out the name of the hotel where we were staying on stage, in one of his songs, and he did it as a kind of present for his boys. He'd always mention his hotel, so the girls would seek him out after the show, but some nights he kept us waiting, and we'd be backstage thinking, Oh, man, tonight is gonna be dead. No one knows where we're staying. But he'd get around to it, eventually. Some nights, they'd send me to remind him, and then when he finally said the name of the hotel, that's when I'd go to work. I'd find the best-looking girls, tell them I was with the tour, and if they didn't believe me I'd flash my All Access pass, along with driver's license, showing where it said "Farmers Boulevard, Hollis, Queens," just to prove I was who I'd say I was. It got me into a lot of places, that driver's license. It made me a big deal, and I was too amped to care that I was only a big deal by extension. Hey, when you're sixteen years old, you'll take it any way you can get it.

My plan, after hanging around these guys for a while, after going to all these shows, a couple times a month, was to get rich by the age of twenty. My idea of rich was a million dollars. I didn't stop to think how I might make that much money, or what I'd do with it once I got it, but that was the figure I had in my head. That was the time frame. Being rich was having a million dollars. Didn't get more specific than that.

>> GONNA PARTY LIKE IT'S 1999

I was a giant Prince fan in high school. He was the man, far as I was concerned. I went through this whole "Purple Rain" phase. I used to take my girlfriends up to my attic. My room was hooked-up, and my mother wouldn't bother me. I'd put on some Prince and make it happen. I think I even had some purple clothes.

Like a lot of guys in my neighborhood, I had it in my head that I would be rich. Million-dollar rich. By the time I hit twenty, though, I started to realize I'd probably be poor for the rest of my life. Scraping. But the Prince thing wouldn't go away, and I readjusted my idea of success to mean that—whatever I was doing, wherever I was doing it—I'd find a way to be at a Prince concert on New Year's Eve, to hear him ring in the year 2000 with that song "1999." It became a pledge I made to myself, and I meant to keep it.

Okay, so I didn't exactly get close on my millionaire-by-twenty pledge. But this one, even if I had to scalp a seat in some nosebleed section for, like, $300, I could probably handle. If that was all the money I had at that time, I'd find a way to be there. That's how much it meant to me as a kid, to be able to party with Prince at the dawn of the next millennium. And that became my new dream, my revised measure of success, to afford a ticket to a Prince concert—not just any Prince concert, but his Y2K New Year's Eve concert, the mother of all concerts.

One thing about Prince, he knew how to market. He knew about branding. I heard him give an interview once, talking about how he knew all along what that song would mean as the 90s came to an end. He said it was a marketing tool, more than anything else, which inspired me all the more. It was seventeen years away, but he knew they'd be playing that song on New Year's Eve, 1999, and it was the first time I realized you could be a genius artist and a genius businessman at the same time. And putting those two impulses together—that was the real genius move.

So here's how it went down—and it was better than any dream I could think up on my own. By 1999, the FUBU thing had happened in a big way. I had money. I had connections. Getting a front-row ticket to Prince's New Year's Eve concert was not going to be a problem. And yet even with all the success I'd had, all the money I'd made, I still thought about this Prince show, this promise I'd made to myself. I'd actually met Prince a couple times, and hung out, and out of nowhere I got this wild invitation to go out to his house in Minnesota to be a guest for this television special he was shooting. Turned out he wasn't going to be performing on New York's Eve, but he had this special in the works, "Rave to the Year 2000," which would be pre-recorded in, like, November, and then dropped like a Dick Clark special on the eve of Y2K.

There were about three hundred people in the audience, and Prince put on a great show, and I got twisted, because of course the world was supposed to end the next day after all our computers crashed, and before he played "1999" he invited me and a couple other people up on stage with him.

I flew onto that stage and started playing air guitar like it was an important part of the show. Like it was my last great act on this earth. There were balloons dropping, and all kinds of excitement, and I was bouncing and sliding about on stage, getting my groove on. I'd never played the guitar in my life, but I was going at it, and as I was playing I thought, Okay, my life is complete. Now I can die.

For months afterwards, I'd get stopped by people in the street, saying things like, "Hey, you're the guy standing next to Prince in that 'Rave to the Year 2000' show!" They didn't know me as the FUBU guy. They didn't know me at all. But they recognized me as this guy on stage, having the time of his life.

Back to high school. My first chance at real money was a little shady. A bunch of my close friends I grew up with started to parlay the money they were making selling drugs into crash cars—vehicles that had been totaled or abandoned and were being offered at auction. There were all kinds of ways to make a hustle from these cars, and pretty soon we'd created a pretty profitable car ring. There was money coming in, money going out. We'd buy the cars at auction, fix them up, and flip them for a nice profit. Or we'd get a car, put some insurance on it, damage it, trade in the parts, and resell the car at the other end. None of us had the time or talent to work on these cars ourselves, but we farmed them out to body shops around town, and there was usually enough money in the deal for me to take out a couple thousand bucks each time I flipped a car.

We had all kinds of scams going, all kinds of cars we'd be working at any one time. Nothing illegal about it, really, except we sometimes wondered where the guys we were buying the cars from got the vehicles in the first place. Eventually, some of the guys I was running with got the idea they'd cut the cost of doing business substantially if they simply stole the cars instead of buying them at auction—and of course, this made sense as a business model, but it wasn't the way I wanted to make *my* living. I didn't judge these friends of mine, for wanting to go down this particular road, but I never went out and stole a car myself, even if I did go along for the ride on a few of these stolen car deals. There was even a crooked FBI agent who crossed our path, at some point early on in this hustle, had us thinking we could jack cars for him at five hundred bucks a pop, and my one buddy who took him up on it ended up applying to the FBI Academy, and being accepted, so I guess the lesson here is that it never hurts to grease the wheel.

Easy money and me, we didn't really get along. I didn't like the hassle, or the headache. Believe me, I liked the making money part, and I thrived on the hustle, but if it came too easy it usually meant we'd cut a few too many corners. It usually meant it was too good to be true. I hated the way I had to look over my shoulder all the time, when one of these deals was going down. I hated that feeling of being exposed, being vulnerable, and I can remember one night, after a particularly lucrative scam, hanging with one of my boys, counting out $90,000 in cash. It was *his* money, *his* scam, but I still couldn't get past the amount. I'd never seen that type of money, all in one place, and I got to thinking, This can't be good. My boy went out and bought himself a brand new BMW, and after that he started going down south and moving a lot of drugs there. Each time he'd get ready to take off on another road trip, I'd say, "How long you gonna keep doin' this, man?" I thought he was being greedy. Sooner or later, it would have to catch up to him, just as sooner or later, the crash cars could come back to bite us. And he'd always say, "Just this one last time."

And of course, *this one last time* kept getting extended, and extended, until eventually the cops nabbed my boy and put him away. Hype Williams ended up making a movie about this guy and a couple of his hustler buddies called "Belly," with DMX and Nas and all these other rap artists, and it was based on the exploits of this crew I was running with, all through high school and just after. My closest friends. Since way back in grade school. But I stayed on the sidelines for all that questionable stuff. Anyway, I meant to. I never stole anything of real value. I never hurt anybody. I never sold drugs, except those few joints I moved that one summer at the YMCA camp upstate. I don't mean to pass myself off as some holier-than-thou type, or some altar boy, because that certainly wasn't the case, it's just that I wasn't cut for this kind of thing. I didn't want to go to jail. I couldn't see being in a cage my whole life. All it took was one night in lock-up to set me straight. All it took was me being in a car with three of my boys and a couple guns when a cop pulled us over. We looked pretty suspicious, four black kids in a car with guns, so they hauled us in. My mother had to come down to get me, and I could see in her eyes how much I hurt her. I didn't want to put her through that again. I respected her too much. I loved her too much. I didn't want to be her disappointment. So I left the serious law-breaking to everyone else, and then one day I looked up and realized I didn't have the time to make any trouble. I was too busy going to school and working my legitimate hustles. Plus, it didn't add up. The space between legal and illegal didn't amount to much. I figured that out early on. I knew guys making the same money working in Church's Fried Chicken as guys dealing drugs. The only difference was the juice, the excitement, and there was enough juice and excitement from the music and the girls and the straight money that I left the other stuff alone.

Absolutely, I ran with a rough crowd, but I was essentially a good kid. I was clean. My thing was, if you want to do something well, you've got to be committed to it. You've got to do it fully. Doesn't matter if it's stealing cars, or selling drugs, or punching the clock on some minimum wage job. You have to focus, one hundred percent. Anything worth doing is worth over-doing, that was my thing. You've got to keep your eye on the prize. That message was reinforced for me, big time, when I took a job at First Boston as a foot messenger during my junior year of high school. I got the job through a co-op program at my school, and the deal was I'd go to school one week and then go to work the next, at the main office in midtown Manhattan. I went in thinking I'd learn all about investment banking, but that wasn't how it played out at all. The real lesson came in studying the thirty or forty other messengers they had working in the mail room. I got to know a lot of these guys really well. There were some real hustling street types, like the guys I'd been running with in and around Hollis. There were some aspiring Wall Street types, hoping to get a leg up and an inside, bottom-floor look at the workings of First Boston. And there were the people who fell somewhere in between, who didn't really know what they wanted out of this job, or where they wanted to go next. Of course, there were also some people who had maxed out on this right here, and I realized I never wanted to be a 50-year-old foot messenger.

>> NEVER HURTS TO ASK

One of the highlights of my time working as a foot messenger for First Boston was catching a delivery for Donald Trump. This was long before "The Apprentice," but he was a big deal back when I was in high school. He represented everything money and power could buy in a city like New York. He was success personified, and I saw his name on my delivery slip one morning and I was determined to meet him. I mean, this guy had more bling than anyone in my neighborhood, except he wore it on his cars, his boats, his planes, his buildings. Plus, he was a kid from Queens, just like me, so I had to see for myself what made this guy tick.

Even then, I could see this guy had it going on. I was fascinated at the way he put his stamp on something so straightforward as real estate. I mean, one high-rise building is a lot like the next one, but every time he put up a building it was distinctive, new, special. Wasn't just because he was slapping his name on the thing in big, bold letters. There was more to it than that. It was Branding 101. Yeah, he had his name on everything, but he made sure his name stood for something.

And so off I went to Trump Tower, determined to meet the master. I walked over to the private elevator bank that led to his office suite, and was met by these beefy, 300-pound, brick-eating security guys, in shiny black suits. I told these guys, with just enough confidence to think I might pull it off, that I wouldn't be able to drop off the package unless Donald Trump signed for it himself. "I have to take it up to Mr. Trump personally," I said.

These brick-eating guys flashed me these steely looks, like I'd just told them I wanted to go out with Ivana, and I never got in to see Donald Trump. His security guys sent me packing. In fact, I can still tell you the kind of wax they used on the floors of Trump Tower in those days, because they shoved me out of there like I was at a bowling alley, and as I slid across that floor on my way to the door I thought, Okay, there's always next time.

(I ended up hanging out with the Donald several times after FUBU hit, so ha ha . . . Can't stop me, baby.)

I tried to study the guys on the receiving end of my deliveries. I'd check out their offices, how they carried themselves, whether they could look a simple messenger like me straight in the eye. You can tell a lot about people by how they treat the people on the lower rungs of the ladder of their life, and I got to thinking that if I had anything to say about it I'd be the guy getting the package and looking the messenger in the eye and taking care of business. That became my focus. The guys I knew in my neighborhood, they were headed for the low-end, but I set my sights high. Hustling was fine, for now, and I would keep hustling for the next while until I could get my footing, but I told myself I'd have to *really* hustle, and focus, and rededicate myself if I meant to reach the other side of the transaction.

RISE

I blew right past twenty no richer than I was at fifteen. I looked up one day and not a whole lot had changed. I was still living in Hollis, still working a bunch of different jobs, still hanging with my boys, still figuring some kind of next move. It was like a holding pattern, and I was one of the only ones standing still. A lot of my friends from the neighborhood had scattered—some went to college, some moved out of town, some were in jail, some were dead—but I kept in close touch with Carl, and J, and Keith. Carl was working in a factory. J joined the Navy and went off to fight in Desert Storm. Keith was managing some apartments in the city. And me, I was treading water.

I thought I knew everything, but of course I had a lot to learn. I had my crash car business going, but it wasn't really going anywhere. I went from thinking it would make me rich, to thinking it could keep me whole, to thinking if I could just keep from getting into trouble over it I was doing okay. I'd set the bar pretty low, I realize now, to count myself a success just because I was keeping out of jail, but that was the standard of the neighborhood. That was what we knew.

The hassle of the hustle, it got to be a real strain. My thing was I'd work a straight, legit job, with a hustle on the side. I was always scrambling. Always scratching. Always waiting for some other shoe to drop, dealing in what I knew might be stolen merchandise even if I didn't steal it myself. It was no way to make a meager living. Of course, if I could have made a killing at it, I wouldn't have cared about the questionable ethics, or the hassle, but since it was a tough go I turned my sights elsewhere. For a while, I had a petty scam working to keep me in pocket money, and I mention it here to show those low standards in full force, and how desperate I was to get a leg up. My barometer was that I didn't want to get caught doing something I wasn't supposed to be doing. It was never any kind of ethical dilemma with me; it was a matter of trying to put one over, and not getting caught, and doing what I could to avoid another one of those disappointed looks from my mother. That just killed me. I never wanted to see that look again—and that's really what kept me honest, more than anything else.

If I thought I could get away with something, I was all for it, like this idea I had to cut the corners off a stack of singles and replace them with the corners from another stack of twenties, and then pass off the doctored bills to street vendors and merchants and hope to get away with the switch. I can't take full credit for this one. Some idiot tried to slip me one of these funny twenties when I was working the popcorn stand at the Coliseum Mall, early on in high school, so I guess I thought I'd balance the scales. The way it worked was I'd rip one corner off a good twenty and stash the small piece away. Then I'd pass the twenty at a bodega, and nobody ever cared if a corner was missing; the bill was still good. When I'd stockpiled enough corners, I went to work on the singles, and when I had enough of these I was in business. I'd buy a soda from a hot dog cart vendor, hand him the bogus bill, and hope like hell he was too busy to notice. Or some guy selling flowers on the street. Those crazy flower-buying days, like Mother's Day and Valentine's Day, that was like taking candy from a baby. I'd see a guy at a street light, selling roses for a dollar, and I'd hand him the bill, get my change and my rose, and peel away before he could notice the funny money. Sometimes, I'd buy myself a nice new pair of sneakers, and I'd put a real twenty on top, three fake twenties in the middle, and a real twenty on the bottom, and hand the money over to the kid working the cash register and wait for my change.

About ninety-five percent of the time, I'd get back sixteen or eighteen dollars in change for my one-dollar investment, or whatever it worked out to be, and on top of that I'd get a flower, or some Chinese food, or a soda. The merchandise was like a little extra bonus. And when it didn't work, I had an easy out. I ran like hell. The few times the counterfeit twenties went bust, I was able to haul out of that store, or down the street in the other direction, and that was the worst of it. That was my alibi. I didn't have to worry about the cops—or, worse, my mother. I just had to worry about my conscience, and in those days, sad to say, it didn't have too much to say about something like this.

>> A BLANKET OF HISTORY

The numbers were out to get me and my boys.

In 1995, sixteen percent of all African American males in their 20s who did not attend college had spent time in prison. Ten years later, that number was up over twenty percent. Today, more than a third of all black men in their 30s with only a high school education have been incarcerated, while over sixty percent of all high school dropouts have been in jail. And get this: among black dropouts in their late 20s, there are more in prison on any given day (thirty-four percent) than there are working (thirty percent), according to a recent study done at the University of California, Berkeley.

If you believe the statistics, the odds were against me. African-American males have far lower graduation rates than their white male counterparts, especially in urban communities, and a far greater likelihood of winding up in jail. The numbers point to racism, uninvolved parents, and a subculture that doesn't value education or reward hard, honest work. But I never believed in statistics. Nothing was inevitable, far as I was concerned. My circumstances might have had it in for me, but it was up to me to see that I didn't head down the same wrong road as most everyone else in my neighborhood. I wanted something better for myself, something more.

I recently came across a quote from President Lyndon Johnson, delivered to the graduating class of 1965 at Howard University, in which he spoke of the plight of what he called "the American Negro." "Much of the Negro community is buried under a blanket of history and circumstance," he said. "But it is not a lasting solution to lift just one corner of that blanket. We must stand on all sides and we must raise the entire cover, if we are to liberate our fellow citizens."

I hear those words now and I take them to heart. But as a young man, dancing in and out of trouble, I didn't give care about liberating our fellow citizens. I didn't care about lifting other young blacks, or setting a positive example. All I cared about was getting mine, and getting away with it.

After a while, this kind of thing got a little old. It wasn't just about staying out of jail; it was me finally paying attention to the person I was becoming, the choices I was making. About a year out of high school, I realized I couldn't outrun the right thing my whole life, so I stopped passing counterfeit twenties or fixing stolen cars and I took a job at a Red Lobster restaurant. I'd always had a job, but this one had a little bit of upside. I wanted to play it straight, and at the same time find some way to make an honorable living. I didn't have a whole lot of options. College didn't really make sense for me. There was too much money going out, just to keep the house running, to think about taking on a substantial tuition bill. Plus, I needed to do my part, to make sure there was enough money coming in. I needed to work, was what it came down to, and I wanted one of those jobs where I could just leave the work at quitting time, with no worries bouncing around in my head about what I'd have to do the next day, or whether or not I'd get caught for something I may or may not have done. I wanted to be paid with clean money, and I wanted to punch out at the end of the day and not bring anything home with me from work other than a plate of fried shrimp, so the Red Lobster job was perfect. I started out in the kitchen, but I ended up waiting tables. That's where the real money is, for a hired hand in the restaurant game, so that's where I put myself.

Around the same time, as a sideline, I bought a van and started driving my own livery route at night, just like I used to do with my mother. The rest of the time I was chasing girls and trying to stay out of trouble. In all, it wasn't a bad set-up, but I was starting to think long-term, to wonder if I could be a waiter at Red Lobster at thirty, if I could still be driving a van, or punching some other clock just to keep the electricity on. I could see I had it better than most, but it wasn't until I hit twenty that I started to think I couldn't do this kind of thing forever.

Meanwhile, the hip-hop scene remained very much a part of our lives, well after high school. It was what we talked about, what we lived for, what mattered most of all. It was more than just the soundtrack to our lives; a lot of times, it was the main storyline. Our weekends were all about going out on these tours, and finding ways to get our expenses covered, or finding ways to make money off the deal. Maybe it wasn't every weekend, but there was always a road trip coming up on the calendar, always something to look forward to. And these shows weren't just a place to get our groove on or let off some steam. They were business opportunities. The artists didn't care if their boys from back home made a little money on the side, so a lot of guys I knew started selling t-shirts outside these concert venues. For a while my big thing was to buy up a whole mess of urban-type clothes—jeans, Timberlands, parkas, sneakers . . . things I wore without thinking about them, which a lot of kids outside New York seemed to associate with our hip-hop culture. I didn't plan on doing this, or think it through, but I started to realize that everywhere I went outside of the city, kids wanted to buy whatever I was wearing, right off my back.

First time it happened, it freaked me out. Some kid offered me a lot of cash for this bomber jacket I was wearing, and I realized I could replace it for half what he was offering me, soon as I got back home. I thought, Done. And then I thought, Well, if this kid wants my jacket, maybe someone else will want my sneakers, or my jeans. Right away, I started thinking like a wholesaler. You couldn't find some of this stuff in Atlanta, or Orlando, or Kansas City, or wherever, so I started bringing along a couple extra pieces before each road trip. It got to where I'd load up two or three suitcases with this stuff and try to move it all in the parking lot before each show, and with each sale I got to thinking, It's good to be from Queens.

>> THE GEOGRAPHY OF COOL

You could make a nice hustle, trying to anticipate which of our urban, hip-hop trends would catch on in the rest of the country. Truth is, they all caught on eventually, and the market came in timing the eventually. For the first time, running back and forth to these shows on the weekends, I caught myself thinking how you could probably chart this kind of thing. There's a whole formula to it. Something hits in New York, some type of music or clothing or lifestyle item, and a couple months later it'll filter out across the rest of the country. It might hit next in DC, or Philadelphia, before snaking its way down to Atlanta, or Orlando, or Miami, and across to Detroit, or Nashville, or Chicago. Or, maybe it'll pop out in Los Angeles, and spread east, through Vegas, and maybe Houston or Kansas City. And by the time it reaches the heartland, there's something new to replace it, already making some new noise in the big city.

Even now, with cell phones and streaming video and wireless Internet, there's still that lag, between New York and L.A. and the rest of the country. In a world of instant messaging, nothing's instantaneous. It doesn't just happen that a new artist or a new trend breaks out of the city and reaches into middle America. Anyway, it doesn't just happen right away. It takes word-of-mouth, and buzz, and the slow-burn marketing tools promoters have been using for centuries. It takes time.

Kids in Columbus, Ohio, they want to feel like they're on the same cutting edge as kids in New York or Los Angeles. It might take them a minute to catch on to some of this stuff, but when it finally shows up on their radar they want in, and there's money to be made if you're the first one there to sell it to them. I don't care what it is, there's always something new, something hot that you can't get your hands on in Columbus, or wherever, and if you're the first guy who takes the time to get it there you'll usually do well with it. That's what I've tried to do with FUBU and everything that followed from it—to stay out in front of these trends.

Back in the day, it was those bomber jackets everyone in New York was wearing. Or an Adidas track suit. Whatever was in style, I'd ride out to one of these shows and the local kids would want to buy this stuff right off my back. Literally. For two or three times what I'd paid for the item back in New York. It didn't take a genius to see a business opportunity. I started small. I sold what I was wearing. And then after a while I started buying extras. Two or three jackets, a couple pairs of jeans, four or five sweat suits. If I could sell ten pieces before a show, I was doing okay. The key was to make sure you had just enough inventory, and that you weren't stuck with anything you couldn't move. Fila sneakers. Ellesse sneakers. Timberlands. I found that if I left the hang tags on the items, I could get a better price.

The other key was to gauge just how far I'd be from New York, to get some kind of read on what kinds of clothes would be in demand. I'd think what these kids wanted on my last trip through town, and instead of bringing more of the same, I'd bring whatever came next back home. The next big thing, I'd turn them on to that, but in small doses. Like a dealer.

You have to realize, this wasn't any kind of real enterprise. This was just me, generating a little something on the side. And it's not like I brought down a truckload of goods. There was only so much stuff I could load into my van, only so much money I could lay out to buy the stuff in the first place—and besides, I didn't want to spend all my time out in the parking lot, selling clothes. I wanted to party. So I found a balance. I sold enough to pay for my gas, and my food, and to leave a few bucks in my pocket besides. Just enough to remind me that there was more where that came from.

The van was a whole other hassle. I was constantly getting tickets, constantly pouring money into the operation. The cops would harass me. I couldn't remember it being this much of a headache when my mother was driving, but the cops were all over us drivers. You know, I wasn't a legal livery company. I had livery plates, my van was marked and registered, but I wasn't supposed to pick up fares in and around the city bus stops, so they'd write me up all the time. Sometimes just to bust my chops, and sometimes for good reason.

I drove like a crazy man, trying to cover as much ground as quickly as possible, to pick up and drop off as many fares as possible, so they'd write me up for that. At one point, I was carrying a couple thousand dollars in fines. On a good night, I could make about three or four hundred bucks, but I gave most of that back, for gas, tickets, insurance, maintenance on the vehicle. Maybe I'd clear two or three hundred for the week—good money, don't get me wrong, but not enough to think of doing it for any longer than I had to.

The hours were the real killer. I'd run from five in the morning, to catch the early commuters, until ten or eleven o'clock at night. In between, when things were quiet in mid-afternoon, maybe I'd grab a couple hours for myself, to hang with my boys or maybe catch up on some sleep, but it was a hard day, and I had about three years of those hard days before I decided I'd had enough. I needed a break, so I re-upped at Red Lobster and once again the restaurant job became my main thing.

Red Lobster was the perfect counter to the van business. I busted my butt on the floor of the restaurant, waiting tables, but there was no stress, none of the headaches I got picking up fares and dodging those livery regulations, none of the looking over my shoulder that came refurbishing those hot cars. It was a different kind of hustle, and the deeper I got into it, the more hours I worked, the more I realized I would never be a desk-job kind of guy. I liked waiting tables. I liked the action. I liked that every shift was different. 'Course, I didn't want to be a waiter for the rest of my life, but I knew I couldn't sit still. That wasn't me. I couldn't understand how people commuted to the same job every day, pushing the same papers across the same desk for the same paycheck. It seemed like such a drain, working on somebody else's dream. A lot of guys I knew, they were looking to get set up in this or that office, but I never understood that corporate mentality. Never mind that I didn't have the education. Never mind that I couldn't land a desk job in any office in New York City, even if I held a gun to someone's head in Human Resources.

I just couldn't understand how someone could go through the same motions every day and call it a career.

It was one thing to dream about making it big, but to actually go about it with a viable plan . . . that was something else. But then I'd keep hearing this line, back of my head: if you fail to plan then you plan to fail. By the time I hit twenty-two, twenty-three, I was starting to see a lot of the guys I'd grown up with, coming into the restaurant for dinner. They'd gone off to college, and now they were back home, working their first jobs. Red Lobster was a big night out for these guys, and I always felt a little embarrassed, walking over to their table to take their orders. Guys I used to run with. Guys I used to party with. Girls I used to go out with. They were college graduates, and I was taking their orders for fried shrimp and tartar sauce, and hustling them for tips. They'd look at me and go, "Hey, D, how you doin'?" And then they'd do a double-take, because back in high school I was the guy who had the hot clothes. I was the guy with all the girls, the guy who made things happen. And here I was, wearing my silly Red Lobster uniform, making sure they had enough tartar sauce. I'd turn my back and know they were laughing at me, but I tried not to care. And—I'm proud to say—I managed *not* to spit in their food. I spit in a lot of people's food, usually with good reason, but never someone I actually knew.

(Like I said, I set the bar pretty low.)

Money was tight, but there was enough to keep me in what I wanted. When I was about twenty or so, my mother moved out of the house and into Manhattan, and I stayed on and moved in some of my friends. J, Keith, Carl and a couple others. I collected rent. I didn't charge a whole lot, but it was enough so I could stay ahead of our bills. There was heat. There was electric. I held the mortgage on the house, and that got paid, along with the taxes. I was doing alright, going out at night, partying with girls, chilling. We were like a frat house.

I wasn't going anywhere, but things were just fine. For the time being.

>> ONE LESS SHRIMP

File this one under Marketing 101. Or, Too Basic Business Strategies. I'd been working at Red Lobster a couple years. They used to have these regular staff meetings, once a week or so, where they'd tell us about their new promotions, their special drinks, whatever we needed to know from the corporate level to keep our little local place cooking. Usually before the dinner rush, they'd get the wait staff together and go over whatever it was they needed to go over, and on this one night they started telling us about this chain-wide cutback on their Shrimp Scampi orders. They'd always put, say, eleven shrimp in a regular order, and maybe six in an appetizer, and now there was a special corporate directive to cut back to ten and five. They wouldn't change the price, just the shrimp count—and, at the other end, there'd be a little more money to go around out at Red Lobster headquarters.

The deal was, with all those Shrimp Scampi orders, all across the chain, Red Lobster would save a couple million dollars over the course of a year. Just from holding back one shrimp per plate. I sat there in my little Red Lobster outfit thinking, This is a genius move, long as it doesn't come back to bite them. At first I thought for sure our regular Shrimp Scampi customers would notice the change right away, and start complaining, but no one ever noticed. No one ever said a thing. And the company saved a small fortune, just on the back of this one move.

The lesson, to a lowly waiter hoping to become something more than a lowly waiter, was that the little things mean a lot. They add up. It's basic, I know, but it's all-important. Keep one shrimp for yourself, and it's one less shrimp you have to keep in inventory. It reminds me now of another genius move from around the same time, when Pocket Books pushed the price point on their paperback books by four cents. Remember when paperback books were always $4.95, or $5.95? That had long been the industry standard, until some enterprising bean counter at Pocket Books came along and realized the publisher could push that loose change to $.99 and nobody would ever know the difference but their shareholders. And just like that, the standard price of all Pocket paperbacks shot to $4.99, or $5.99, and those extra four cents added up to millions.

Absolutely, it's the little things. Studies show that if you own a retail clothing store, you can bump your business by as much as twenty percent just by placing four comfortable chairs in the middle of your store. Why? Because a lot of women shop with their husbands and boyfriends and kids, and if they have a place to sit down they won't be looking to leave so quickly. The women will have more time to shop and spend money. Makes sense, right? Just like it makes sense to serve one less shrimp, or squeeze an extra few cents from an avid reader, or figure out some other way to grow your business without changing your business model or alienating your core customers.

Bottom line? It doesn't have to be a big deal to amount to a big deal.

Over time, these road trips really forced me to think outside the box, to be entrepreneurial. There was all this money floating around, and I figured if I was smart about it I could redirect a little more of it my way. Selling the clothes off my back was easy enough, and loading up on extras was another no-brainer, but then I realized I could put my van to good use hauling all kinds of merchandise to these concert venues. Around the time of the Rodney King beating, in March, 1991, which sparked the rioting out in Los Angeles in 1992, I printed up a bunch of "Free Rodney King!" t-shirts and drove them down to a march in DC, where I thought I could sell them for ten dollars a pop. Here again, the idea wasn't original to me. A lot of my friends were making good money selling unlicensed t-shirts in the parking lots after concerts, or at sporting events. We've all bought shirts like these, for about half the price of the licensed t-shirts they sell inside the arena. So I went to a place called Eva Tees in Manhattan and bought three hundred blank t-shirts. That was all I could afford. Then I took them out to a screen printer on Long Island, where we laid on some artwork a friend of mine did on the computer. Rodney King's picture, along with our slogan.

It never occurred to me that we needed to pay Rodney King for the use of his likeness. I just grabbed the best photo of him I could find and went to work. Then I loaded up the van with the shirts, drove down to the march, laid a couple samples on the grass and sold through my entire inventory in nothing flat. My only regret was that I didn't have enough money to make more shirts, and I came away with my first lesson in business: sell-through is all-important, but if you misread your market and don't make enough product to meet demand, it can be a real buzz-kill.

Next, I started going to this outlet on 27th Street, and buying all kinds of knock-off goods. Remember those super-soaker water guns? I bought a whole mess of those, and all kinds of other items. Little did I know, a couple years later, me and my FUBU partners would risk our lives trying to bust-up the counterfeiters working out of this same building, but this time I was on the scraping side of the equation. These knock-off goods were my ticket—and not the drag on profits they'd become. I'd buy something for two dollars, and fig-ure I could sell it for five, so I started loading up the van with all this merchandise, and all these clothing items, and hitting the road in search of concerts, and festivals, and trade shows. County fairs. Anywhere there'd be a bunch of people with some loose change that might have my name on it.

One day I took stock and realized these road trips had become a lot more than R&R. I found myself counting on the money I could make from these sideline sales, and I'd catch myself thinking of new t-shirt designs, or other selling opportunities. I went to a bunch of dif-ferent silk screen places back home, comparing prices. And I tried to keep enough cash on hand so I didn't top out at three hundred blank t-shirts next time there was a great selling opportunity coming up on the calendar.

Around this same time, I caught myself looking for a hat I'd seen in a video by this group De La Soul, these three talented guys from Long Island. Like a lot of people in my neighborhood, I was influ-enced by the styles of some of these early rap artists, but the influ-ences were subtle. I don't think any of us realized we were buying these clothes because we'd seen our favorite artists wear the same thing. Or, if we did, we didn't really talk about it. We just grabbed on to this or that trend and called it our own. This was really the first time I was consciously aware of the subliminal power of music videos as a marketing tool, and I was a textbook case. I'd seen this hat, I thought it had flavor, and I went out looking for one to add to my wardrobe. It was a tie-top hat, and I couldn't find one anywhere in New York City. I spent a whole day looking. Brooklyn. Queens. Manhattan. It became a real quest. And when I finally found one, I was disappointed. They were charging like thirty dollars for it, and the thing was so poorly constructed it looked like it wouldn't last but a week.

Remember, I knew how to sew. I was hemming my own pants and making alterations on my clothes since I was a little kid. I knew a flimsy piece of crap when I saw one. But I'd set my mind on that hat, so I bought it anyway, and soon as I got home with the thing I got out my mother's sewing machine and started sewing a couple knock-offs. I wasn't thinking about selling these hats, just that I could follow the pattern and do a better job of it, and at the other end I'd stockpile a few for my own use, because I knew this store-bought one wouldn't last, and because I liked to have options when I got dressed. I used a whole bunch of different colors, so I'd have a hat to match the trim of this sneaker, or the design of that shirt. You might look back at a picture of me from this period—late 80s, early 90s—and think I had this thrown-together look, but it was all about the ensemble, even down to an accessory like a tie-top hat. Everything had to go together, in one way or another.

>> THE TRUTH ABOUT KICKS

Inner city kids are extremely status-conscious. That's a given. We care about our appearance. We care about the cars we drive, the watches on our wrists, the labels we put on our bodies. It says something about us. And this is nowhere more apparent than our footwear. Take me. I didn't have any real money, but I always had a closet full of sneakers. And they all had to be clean. Out-of-the-box clean. If there was a scuff or a mark or a blemish of any kind, the sneakers were of no use to me.

Going back to the earliest days of hip-hop, sneakers were our thing. There was even a term in the hip-hop community for guys who took this stuff a little too seriously—"sneakerheads". We used to braid our shoelaces a certain way. Or make little checkerboard design patterns on them. I used to stay home Friday nights and clean the things with a toothbrush. So when I finally had a little bit of money, it went right to my feet. There's a joke here, how people say money goes to your head, but where I grew up it was just the opposite. Soon as I could afford it, I started buying six, seven, eight pairs of sneakers at a time.

And it wasn't just sneakers. Back in my Red Lobster days, I was buying a new pair of Timberlands every two or three weeks. They didn't wear out; they just got dirty. Even today, I'll check out someone's closet and see a couple hundred pairs of shoes in there. Sneakers, mostly. And most of them are in good shape, except for a scuff mark here or there. That's enough to get them "retired".

You look at the ridiculous success of some of these footwear companies, like Nike, and you can

draw a straight line to the repeat buys from the
African-American community. It's the same five to
ten percent of their customers buying the majority
of their shoes. Just look back at the recent history
of a company like Reebok, a time-tested, successful brand that kind of disappeared for a while until
they hired Peter Arnell and Steve Stout, an established marketing guru and a music executive looking to change the advertising world, and started
targeting the African-American market. Until
artists like Jay-Z and 50 Cent signed on for a full-
fledged ad campaign, joining athletes like Allen
Iverson, and all of a sudden black kids started buying them up in bunches.

Pollsters are always saying that voters or consumers decide with their feet, but here it rings
especially true.

Soon, a couple friends wanted to know if I could make a hat for
them, so I turned out a few more. It was easy enough, just a piece
of fabric cut into a simple square. Then I'd sew a lining on it, and take
two of these finished squares and sew them together. Boom, you
have a hat, and you tie it on the top and you're good to go. The first
few hats I made were solid colors, but then I started reaching for
some stripes, some patterns. Whatever fabric I thought looked good
or felt nice. I went to the fabric store and bought some material.
Nothing too expensive. The cost of goods for each hat was less
than a dollar, and each one took only a ten or fifteen minutes to
make, and once I started making them in bigger numbers the costs
and the production time came way down.

It's probably useful to put my developing fashion sense into some kind of context. In the world of hip-hop or urban clothing, or whatever you want to call it, there were a couple fixtures. There was Brand Jordan at Nike, and that "sneaker lure" was able to build a whole line of warm-ups, tops, jackets, ball caps and related items. You couldn't really say those items were made for the black community, but there's no denying that they were embraced by the black community. There was Tommy Hilfiger, which didn't seem to target blacks either. Later on, a rumor would surface that Tommy Hilfiger didn't make his clothes to fit black people, but nevertheless the line made its first piece of real noise when a rapper named Grand Puba started talking about it in his rhymes. *Tommy Hilfiger on my back . . . that's just my flava.* The same artist also threw a couple shout-outs to Girbaud Jeans, and these were really the first big designer logo rises of our urban culture. There were bigger artists out there, but outside of Run-DMC with Adidas, no one was dropping these brand names in their songs in such a "product placement" type of way. No one was making these markets.

When I started sewing these first couple hats, there was a company called Cross Colours on the scene, and they were making clothes out of Kinte cloth colors that called to mind the batik patterns of certain African tribes. Plus, the texture of the fabric itself was unique, almost like a lightweight burlap, and you started to see black people walking around in orange jeans and purple jean jackets. I'd always been into sewing, and doctoring my own clothes, so I was really excited by this development. I used to check out the clothes in the stores, and consider the quality, and see if there were some elements I could layer on to the clothes I already had. I couldn't really afford to buy the items outright, but I wanted the look.

All of a sudden, that "look" was everywhere. Big stars like Danny Glover and Whoopi Goldberg would show up on red carpets and talk shows wearing Cross Colours, and next thing you know everyone was wearing it. Our clothes started to get baggier, and more colorful.

Designers like Karl Kani, who came out of Cross Colours, began to really put a stamp on hip-hop culture. The Cross Colour guys were hot, but Karl Kani was fire. He was from Brooklyn. He looked like a young Mike Tyson. He put his name on his clothes, and it hit me like a bolt of lightning, that somebody like me could make a name for himself making clothes.

The Troop line was huge for a while, but there was no personal connection there, the way there was with Karl Kani. LL Cool J was a big wearer of Troop, which was a Korean-owned company, but almost as soon as that line popped in a giant way there was a rumor on the street that the company's name stood for To Reign Over Oppressed People. It sounds ridiculous now, but that rumor killed the line. The Koreans didn't understand their market, and couldn't think how to respond. They used to make those leather jackets that every-body was wearing, and they just disappeared, and even a waiter at Red Lobster could see the importance of building and sustaining pos-itive relations with your core consumers if you hoped to build and sustain any kind of real business.

Meanwhile, I kept selling my hats. Friends of mine started asking me where they could get a hat like that for themselves, and then I started hearing from friends of friends, and after that I started think-ing maybe I should make a couple dozen and see if I could sell them at some of these concerts. I closed my eyes and saw that giant can opener my mother used to keep on the wall of our house and reminded myself to think big. I thought, why stop at making this stuff for me and my friends?

>> THE RIPPING POINT

One of the biggest controversies in the world of urban apparel had nothing to do with an urban line of apparel—at least not in any kind of traditional sense. See, in the hip-hop community, some of our earliest fashion choices were taken off the racks of conservative, white-owned companies like Lacoste, Ralph Lauren and Timberland. That was what was out there, and available. If we saw something we liked, we reached for it, put our own stamp on it, and adopted it as our own.

In my neighborhood, Timberland boots were the coolest. They weren't made for us, necessarily, but we didn't care. We didn't eat granola or hike or read *Outside* magazine, same way Gucci or Burberry didn't make items for our particular lifestyle. But we liked our Timberlands. I always had a new pair in my closet, ready to go when the previous pair got a little scruffy. I liked the way they set off the cuff of my jeans, liked the way they fit, liked that they represented an outdoor lifestyle. Back then, I didn't give the fact that it was a white-owned company a thought, because if I only spent my money on stuff made and marketed by black-owned companies, there wouldn't have been a whole lot for me to buy.

We were all color-blind when it came to clothes. We liked what we liked, until one day when some Timberland executive came out and said they didn't make their boots for drug dealers. Their sales were through the roof, and they could see that inner city kids were driving those sales, but with this one statement they alienated a core group of their consumers. They nearly killed their business—and, unwittingly, started a fashion revolution, because it was this misstep by Timberland that inspired me to launch a company like FUBU. They did more than just alienate us. They ticked us off, and we went from thinking Timberland could do no wrong to writing the company off entirely.

Almost overnight, sales of Timberland boots flat-lined in our urban communities, while Timberland executives scrambled to cover their butts and recapture some of those lost sales. They weren't talking about all black kids, they tried to have us believe. The comments were taken out of context, they assured. They welcomed the attention from rap and hip-hop artists in their songs and videos, they assured.

They even launched some lame damage-control campaign urging people to "give racism the boot"—a clever tag line, given the circumstances, but we weren't buying it. They put up all these billboards, in all these ghetto communities, with a big picture of a boot. That was their clean-up campaign, but they were a little slow on the switch. If these guys thought their hardcore, white-bread customers would be put off by having all these rappers and "gangsters" walking around in the same pair of shoes, then we didn't want any part of them, no matter what they put up on those billboards. And it wasn't like there was a meeting or anything, and every black kid voted to wear something else. It took on a momentum all its own, because when you're style-conscious and status-conscious, this kind of thing finds you. We were out-raged, and wounded, and for the first time I realized the power of this marketplace. Cater to us, and we'll follow you anywhere. Reject us and we'll drive you into the ground.

So there was all this noise about Timberland bouncing around my head, all these thoughts about branding and marketing and finding a way to connect with your customers beyond the product itself, all these positive connections to a guy like Karl Kani and the bolt of lightning that told me you could be young and hip and black and still find a way to develop a line of clothes. I read a lot of books. My favorite, "Think and Grow Rich," I try to read at least once a year. It taught me to write down my goals and to read them back every morning and every night. It also taught me desire, which the author says is the key to everything else. My thing here in this book is power, but you can't have power without desire. The one follows from the other, and this was how I was thinking all the way back then.

There was a lot to think about, and it occurred to me that if I was going to sell these hats I should probably come up with a name. I should associate myself with these goods in some way beyond the simple transaction. It was different than those silk-screened t-shirts, because back then nobody bought a t-shirt and paid attention to the label, but I knew that young people were really into labels and the stature that came with them and I thought I could create something bigger than just a duffel bag filled with tie-top hats. I thought I could make a business.

I think I was probably drunk at the time, but I've since realized that being clear-headed has nothing to do with clarity of vision. Truth be told, I had some of my best ideas when I was out partying with my friends, and the first of these came one night at my house on Farmers Boulevard, just sitting around with Keith, Carl, J and them, drinking, talking about what we might do next. I was all excited about these tie-top hats, and I guess my mind was working in a kind of Timberland backlash mode, because I blurted out the phrase, "By Us, For Us." Don't know where it came from precisely, don't know what the conversation had been leading up to this moment, but I liked it as soon as I heard it back. *By Us, For Us*. It had a certain pride of ownership to it, a certain simplicity. It commanded respect. And I don't know that I recognized it as such at the time, but it was a little bit of a rebuttal to what was going down with Timberland. No, those boots weren't made for us, but these hats would be. Hats, shirts . . . whatever came next. We *were* the market we intended to serve, and the name reinforced the point.

The bonus was that it came with a cool acronym. At least, we all *thought* it was cool, that first drunken night. BUFU. *By Us, For Us*. It was strong, in-your-face, memorable. I was thinking of a guy like Karl Kani, how in a short time he had become so completely identified with his clothes, like it was a real pride of stewardship thing. He put himself in his ads. He put his name on his clothes. I thought I could rope my friends into whatever business I could build on the back of these hats, and that we'd put ourselves in our ads, and we'd put our name on our clothes, too. That was my loose plan.

I went out and printed up a bunch of "BUFU" labels at a silk screener I was using, and a week or so later some guy came up to me on the street and asked me if I was gay. I'd sewn one of the labels into one of my hats and taken it out for a trial run. I thought, Where is that coming from?

He said, "You know what that means?" He was from down south, and spoke with a thick accent.

I said, "By us, for us. It's the name of my new company."

He said, "No, that's not what it means."

I thought, Oh, damn. Now what do we do? Still, I liked the name and the concept behind it too much to scrap it entirely, so I switched it around to FUBU—*For Us, By Us*. I had some new labels printed up, and on the Friday afternoon before Easter Sunday, 1991, I took a small bag stuffed with forty hats to the Coliseum Mall at 165th Street and 89th Avenue in Jamaica and went to work. My boy Keith came along to help me out. We didn't have a permit. We didn't have a strategy. We just stood out there in front of the mall, pretty much on the same spot I used to stand back when I was a kid, handing out fliers for the flea market, and started slinging my hats. Turned out we were standing next to a couple guys who ended up calling themselves the Shabazz Brothers, who were also selling tie-top hats, and who would go on to develop their own line of urban clothing, but I tried not to let the competition bother me. I actually liked their hats a little better than mine. They were of better quality. But there was room enough on that street for all of us. And there were a couple elements in that Shabazz Brothers hat I could incorporate into my FUBU line when I went back into production—so it was my first experience checking out the competition and seeing if I could do my job any better.

We ended up selling every last hat, for twenty bucks a pop. Took just a couple hours for our sell-through. That came to eight hundred dollars, which to a hustling street kid like me was more money than I'd ever come by honestly in a day's work. Okay, so there were two of us out there hustling, and it was a little more than a day's work, if you count shopping for the fabric, and sewing the hats, and the fact that I must have sunk in about forty or fifty dollars in materials, but still . . . eight hundred dollars! We raced back to my car, and I sat down in the driver's seat and counted the money all over again. I thought, I can do this every week. I did the math and grew rich in my head. I kept the money in my lap as I pulled away, and I counted it again. In fact, I was counting the money as I turned my first corner on the way home, and I was so distracted I rear-ended the guy right in front of me. Ended up costing about eight hundred dollars to fix his car, so just like that the money was gone. I thought, Easy come, easy go.

>> SAME STORY, DIFFERENT DECADE

Everything old is new again.

As I write this, in the summer of 2006, there's a new storm brewing about the "unwelcome attention" brought on a staid, status-oriented brand. Cristal, the high-end champagne that had been the bubbly of choice among rappers, which sells for as much as $1,000 a bottle and had lately been featured in raps and videos and episodes of MTV's "Cribs," came out and disassociated itself from the black community.

You'd think these guys might learn from each other's mistakes. For years, artists like Jay-Z, Snoop Dogg, Notorious B.I.G., P. Diddy and 50 Cent had been rapping about Cristal and pumping it up. It flowed like water backstage, and in the hottest clubs, and by all accounts had leapfrogged over its competitors to become the industry standard. And then all of a sudden the managing director of Cristal, a racist idiot named Frederic Rouzaud, came out and said he wasn't interested in sales to young blacks. Apparently, our money isn't quite as green as everybody else's, and he suggested all the shout-outs for his brand might actually hurt sales long-term, despite the recent bump.

I heard this and thought, What's wrong with these people? All you have to do is go into almost any club in almost any city and you'll see Cristal selling like crazy. It's like the Maybach Mercedes of sparkling wine—and priced accordingly. And yet according to the great minds at Cristal, there's a taint to our business, to where they could dismiss our interest in their brand as a "curiosity."

"What can we do?" this year's idiot told *The Economist*. "We can't forbid people from buying it. I'm sure Dom Perignon or Krug would be delighted to have their business."

Yeah, I'm sure they will, just as I'm sure Frederic Rouzaud and his ignorant colleagues will want to forget the day they turned their backs on our money—while me and my boys pop open a bottle of Dom and toast our success.

Right away, Jay-Z put it out that he was boy-cotting Cristal, and next thing you knew no one from our community would touch the stuff. All of a sudden, you had all these bottles, stacking up in retail, and they just weren't moving, to where they'd soon have to be discounted. All the clubs started pouring other brands. In just one day, a bottle of Cristal on your table went from symbolizing pros-perity, culture and accomplishment to representing ignorance and supporting the racists of today.

I went out a couple more times to the Coliseum, hats in hand, and tried to repeat the success of that first outing. I made a few mod-ifications to my design, each time out. Sometimes I got close to that first sell-through, sometimes I fell far short. Sometimes, it was freezing out there, and there was nothing in the way of foot traffic so no real way for me to tap any real sales. But after a while I started seeing my hats around town. I'd see that little FUBU label and get all excited.

I decided to branch out into t-shirts. I had some designs made up—one with FUBU in a distinctive script; the other a stylin' FB logo—and looked to silk screen them on shirts, hoping to make a little money and to reinforce the brand. Remember, this was 1991, and clothing companies were starting to put their names in big, bold letters on almost everything they made. It's like it was no longer enough to get the kids to buy the merchandise in the first place, but now they had to do your advertising for you. So I bought into that, and hoped like hell there'd be some customers willing to buy into it right along with me. I went back to that same screen printer I'd used for those first Rodney King t-shirts, same guy who did my labels for me, and I discovered a place where I could get blank t-shirts for a dollar. They were seconds, but they were nice enough. I even went out and found three professionals in the embroidery business, Bob, Andrea and Gary, and started embroidering our logos on these shirts, which really made them stand out. No one was doing embroidery in those days, so it was a good way to distinguish the brand.

I also bought my first ad around this time—a full page in *Right On!* magazine, which set me back about $3,000. (My mother's friend Larry Grossberg helped us to negotiate that discounted rate.) A couple friends went in on it with me, and we started getting calls from all over the world. Japan, of all places. I'd gotten a credit card machine, and I had to pay a ridiculous fee in order to process a transaction, but I saw it as a sign that I had arrived. And the orders came in. We were moving about fifty hats a week, for a couple months, all on the back of this one ad.

Next, I took a booth at the Black Expo, at the Jacob Javits Center in Manhattan. I thought I'd kick things up a notch. The Black Expo was like a large scale swap meet featuring all kinds of African-American owned companies selling their stuff, or mainstream companies looking to reach into the African-American community. Soap companies, car companies, insurance companies . . . Coca-Cola had a booth. AT&T had a booth. These big companies used the Expo as a forum to launch new products, while smaller companies looked to make their first splash on the cheap. I used to go there as a consumer, and I'd see all these clothing guys, selling product. The show before, there was a lot of Kinte cloth on display, and I thought this stuff was about to pop in a big way.

The Expo was like a tricked out flea market, with a little bit of everything. It really ran the gamut, so I bought a booth for a couple hundred dollars. I had a friend spray-paint a back drop for me, and I set it up behind a couple tables and called it a booth. A lot of these established companies had really professional booths, all organized and glamorous, but I was content with my bridge table and FUBU backdrop. We might have looked like a band of amateurs, but hundreds of kids came seeking us out, looking for our shirts.

The interesting thing about these first few batches of shirts was that they were the only product we ever made that told our full story. *For us, by us.* We had that printed on the back. We had FUBU on the front, in a dictionary style, with the hyphen and the pronunciation and everything. Just like an entry in Webster's. And then on the back we spelled it out, and that's the only time we've ever done that, on any item issued by our company. Those five thousand or so shirts, from those first few Black Expos, they're the only ones that carried the whole legend. And it got around. People knew what it meant. People started to ask for us. Whatever we'd done, we'd done it right. We had a hot line, the embroidered shirts especially. The tie-top hats eventually faded away, that style didn't last, but I ordered a bunch of baseball caps and started putting our logo on that, and those were pretty popular.

Whatever we were putting out there, people wanted in.

SHOW

I couldn't run this operation from the back of my van forever. After those first couple sell-throughs at concerts and marches and Black Expos, and after dipping my toe in the waters of direct mail advertising, I realized I needed to get it together if I meant to grow this "business" beyond a one-shot operation. I needed to incorporate. I needed to trademark the FUBU name and logo. I needed to find some way to streamline my efforts.

I registered the FUBU name, as a DBA—*doing business as*. That was the cleanest way to play it, at that early stage. I dug deep and paid for a lawyer, to dot all the *i*'s and cross all the *t*'s. I developed a business plan—a loose plan, to start, but it was a place to begin. I also brought in my boys as partners. There was me, J, Carl, Keith and one other guy. That one other guy, he came and went. We tried a few different guys in that role. Whoever it was, he was like the fifth Beatle. He'd work with us a while, lose interest and drop out. The next guy would work with us a while, lose interest and drop out. It was always someone with a short-term view. One week, it was some guy who wanted to be a rapper. Then it was some guy who wanted to be an actor. Always, there was something better out there—or so each one of these guys thought. It was just as well. Who wants to hang around chickens when you're hoping to fly like an eagle?

The four of us, though, we stuck with it. It was a sideline for each of us, so we stuck with it as far as our schedules allowed. We made it as much of a priority as we could. I kept my job at Red Lobster and worked my FUBU business around my shifts. A couple weeks in there, I don't think I had time to sleep. I thought, *I'll sleep when I'm dead*. The pipe dream was to open our own boutique, where we could sell our own clothes and some other independent lines. That was the pot of gold at the end of the rainbow, and we were a long way off. Short of that, we wanted to get our clothes in some local stores, maybe even get a department store display. In the meantime, we sold our shirts at every Black Expo in driving distance of New York. Philadelphia, Washington DC, Boston. There was usually a show every month or so. In between Expos, we continued to hit the concert circuit and do some selling there, if we thought it made sense. We got to be fairly well known. Anyway, our clothes got to be well known. They had a certain style to them, a certain flavor. And the concept behind our entire line—young guys from the neighborhood putting out comfortable, affordable clothes for other young guys from the neighborhood—seemed to hit with a lot of people. We put it out there, and it caught on, to where people didn't mind handing over twenty or thirty bucks to us for a nice t-shirt because it was like putting money back into their own community, because we offered something of value in return. Really, these were nice shirts, an easy sell at an easy price point, and soon enough we had some of our boys wearing them in the clubs, and that just reinforced the brand.

We did about six of these Expos in a stretch of two years, and each time we brought more and more inventory. Each time, we tried to do a little something new, to push things in some new direction. Different styles, different looks, different colors. And people came looking for us. We couldn't keep our clothes in stock, that's how much buzz there was attached to our product. Can't say for sure where the buzz came from, those first couple shows, but it came. We were too busy handling the mess of details getting ready for each Expo. It took time to design and print the shirts, to carry the goods back and forth from our suppliers, to make our booth look a little nicer each time out.

'Course, I know full well the buzz didn't happen all by itself. Without really realizing it, we did what we could to help it along. We didn't think of it as marketing or branding or advertising, didn't even think of it as a strategy, but we kept pushing the line in every way available to us. We wore our clothes ourselves, out at the clubs and at concerts, so we became our own walking billboards. We got our friends to wear our stuff, too, and since New York was the center of our universe and the locus of hip-hop culture, a lot of our friends were starting to make some noise of their own, so it worked out well for us that as all eyes were starting to fix on them they were fixing on our t-shirts at the same time.

At some point early on, we branched out into hockey jerseys, which were just becoming hot. Chris Latimer, a well-known promoter on the hip-hop scene who consulted for CCM, the biggest hockey jersey company in North America, was getting all these rappers to wear his jerseys, so I followed his lead and bought a bunch of blanks from CCM. I told them I coached in a youth league, or some line of bull, because they wouldn't sell it to me if they knew the intended use, and they shipped me the blanks with the colors of the current NHL teams. I worked with the color scheme on each jersey and added some nice FUBU elements. Big block letters. Embroidery. Whatever I could sprinkle on those jerseys to make them distinctive, something a kid would want to wear for a night on the town.

More and more, as I was putting myself out there and dealing with manufacturers and shipping people and lawyers and designers and whoever the hell I had to deal with to get FUBU off the ground, I started to realize how important it was for me to be able to communicate with all types of people, from all kinds of backgrounds. Black, white, Asian, Hispanic . . . you had to get along with everyone, especially in the garment industry. Gay and straight. Christian, Jewish and Muslim. College-educated and high school dropouts. I knew as much going in, and it was fairly obvious we'd have to draw on talented people from a variety of backgrounds, but it was something I had to pay attention to just the same. I was working with people of every conceivable stripe, from every conceivable station, and I was determined to do a decent job of it. The key was looking past those stripes, and getting along.

>> TRUE COLORS

Wasn't always easy, being color blind. Wasn't always easy, looking beyond our obvious differences to find common ground. Growing up, the only white people I came into contact with were authority figures. Cops. Teachers. Doctors. People who were always talking down to me, in one way or another. And without really realizing it we were taught to take it, to have to shoulder all this disregard and disrespect just because of the color of our skin.

I wasn't raised that way, but it was the way of the street. Hell, it was the way of the world. And it came up, when we were getting the business going. Absolutely, it came up. And whenever it did

I was reminded of an exchange I had back in my neighborhood with my mother's boyfriend Steve. He had a good sense of people. He came into my life when I was about twelve. And he's still an important part of my life. He went with me one day to the bike store, so I could pick up some parts for this little bicycle repair business I had going, and he started up some small talk with the owner. Me and my boys were in that store all the time, and the guy who ran the place was always nice enough, but this was Steve's first time. The bike store owner heard where Steve was from and replied, "Oh, yeah, a white man can run free up there."

It was a tossed off comment, meant nothing to me at twelve, but Steve heard it for what it was. He knew right then this guy was cut from different cloth. Didn't matter that I'd been a good customer. Didn't matter that this man had chosen to make his living in a black community. Didn't matter that I'd thought he was cool, or that we were cool with each other.

Right there, right in front of this guy, Steve turned to me and said, "Daymond, don't ever come into this man's store again. He disrespects your race. He's making money off you and your friends and he couldn't care less about you." There was no anger in his voice, no rancor—but there was no nonsense, either.

We marched out of there, and I never set foot in that shop again, but I've thought about that moment often. I've thought about how I was so easily fooled by this bigot passing for tolerant. I've thought about how important it is to give someone the benefit of the doubt on these racial issues, but to be keenly aware of what you get back in return. I've thought how sometimes a flash of prejudice can take a real subtle form, and how it's that first flash that can blow up on you and do the most damage.

And I've thought about my mother's boyfriend Steve, who happened to be white. Yeah, I know, I forgot to mention that at the top of this piece, but that's only because I forgot to notice . . . until just now.

Around the time of our launch, the country started getting a little smaller, in terms of music and reach and pop-cultural phenomenon. We didn't plan on it, didn't anticipate it, didn't really notice while it was happening, but that's what happened. Anyway, that was my read. Throughout the 1980s, when rap was establishing a foothold on the music scene, the main influences were mostly regional. You had your East Coast rappers and your West Coast rappers, and a couple groups in-between. You had artists like Run DMC and LL Cool J in New York; NWA in Los Angeles; Luke in Miami; the Ghetto Boys down in Texas, and on and on. Maybe four or five regions, all across the country, setting the tone in terms of rap and hip-hop, and there was very little crossover from one region to the next. Kids in New York didn't listen to music out of L.A., not in any kind of big way, although kids in L.A. had no choice but to listen to what was coming out of New York, because truth be told that's where it was at. Kids in the heartland listened to some watered-down, politically correct version of rap and hip-hop. But that all started to change, as FUBU came of age. All of a sudden, artists were on a level playing field. DJs started spinning their records, no matter where they were from, and that opened up the country in a big way. Not just in music, but in movies, in fashion, in business . . . across the board. Karl Kani was being sold in Macy's, just to give you an idea how mainstream we were about to become. LL was developing a sitcom for CBS. And for the first time the Top 40 pop charts were shot-through with rap and hip-hop.

So that was the mood of the room, the mood of the country, and it hit me that the way to tap into this new landscape was through television. Wasn't such a genius idea at the time. I mean, big companies had been advertising on prime time network television for decades, but we didn't have prime time network television kind of money. Hell, we didn't have any money. Whatever we made went straight to rent, or right back into materials for our next run. Or I'd spend it on gas and tolls and a new set of tires. The genius move, if there was one, was to tap into our target market on the cheap—mainly, through music videos. It was like guerilla product placement, the way these rap and hip-hop artists could start or validate a trend simply by wearing a certain type of outfit or mentioning a brand in one of their lyrics.

It was so obvious to me, the power of this new art form—and yet, for whatever reason, it didn't appear obvious to anybody else. Weren't a whole lot of people doing what we were doing, looking to bust out on the back of the music business, and before I even realized it we had kind of eased our way onto the video scene. Very quickly, music videos had become our CNN, our *Newsweek*, our bulletins from the front. Music videos and BET—that's how we stayed in touch with each other, and on top of each new trend.

Back then, Ralph McDaniels was one of the most respected

promoters of rap and hip-hop in our community—a real maven, in every sense of the term. He's still a force on local radio in New York, but in the middle 1980s he was one of the first people playing rap and hip-hop music videos in the city, back when MTV wouldn't touch this type of music. He had a one-hour show every afternoon, and it's impossible to underestimate the influence of that one show. For the first time, you could see young black people on television who weren't drug dealers or basketball players. It was a huge deal, to see kids just like us, making it big, or about to make it big, on the back of something positive like music. Everybody we knew watched Ralph McDaniels, so I followed him down to some event in Virginia one summer weekend, thinking I could give out some shirts and maybe get some coverage on his show. It was a no-brainer, and I ended up giving a bunch of shirts to Ralph McDaniels, and he ended up interviewing me on his show. He's a good guy, and we hit it off. That was the first time any of us were interviewed on behalf of FUBU, and as soon as that thing aired we started getting calls from stores all over the city, wanting to carry our line. You could chart the cause-and-effect. Trouble was, we weren't set up to supply these stores in any kind of big-time way. Some of them operated on a COD basis, and that would kind of keep the FUBU engine running, but most of them did business on consignment, which meant we suddenly had all this inventory out there with no money coming back in. It was a real drain on our cash flow. With the Expos and concerts and stuff, we were used to selling through our line and plowing the profits back into the next run, but here we were stretching ourselves pretty thin.

Ralph McDaniels had a lot of things going on. He was a true promoter. He was into all kinds of fashion shows and events. He gave many of today's artists their start, and hip-hop owes him a tremendous debt. Mary J. Blige. Puff Daddy. LL Cool J. He was like the Ed Sullivan of our world, always spotlighting these young performers, trying to get them the attention they couldn't find on mainstream outlets like MTV, attention he felt they deserved, and he took a liking to us. He liked our clothes. He liked what we were about. He put us on the map, really, at least in New York, and other than the small problem of trying to figure out how to keep ahead on these consignment sales, we were really rolling.

Meanwhile, my boy Hype Williams started making a name for himself as a music video director (Ralph McDaniels gave him his start as well), and I started going down to his sets with a bunch of shirts, hoping to convince one of the artists or one of the dancers to wear them in the shoot. I didn't think this all the way through, to what it might mean for our business, but it was clear even to me that getting these young artists to wear our clothes in their videos could only be a good thing. I mean, putting one of my shirts on LL Cool J and seeing him wear it onstage . . . that was thrill enough, one of the best feelings in the world, and on top of that it created a huge demand for our clothes.

>> AMERICAN BRANDSTAND

Check this out: in the first-half of 2004, there were a total of 62 songs that had spent time in the Billboard Top 20 singles chart. Twenty-seven of those songs, or 44 percent, contained at least one branded reference, amounting to 645 branded references in all, according to a report issued by Agenda Inc., a San Francisco-based consulting company. That works out to about ten references per song. High-end brands like Cadillac, Hennessy, Gucci and Rolls Royce are typically the most cited by hip-hop artists, but mainstream brands like Geico, Bank of America, Toys R Us and Avis also make the cut. And in each and every case, these mentions correspond to a huge bump in revenues for the companies involved.

For some reason, the trend seems to begin and end in this one segment of the music industry. Over the same period, the only non hip-hop song in the Billboard Top 20 to contain a brand reference was Jessica Simpson's "With You," which talked about her Levi's. What this means is that rap and hip-hop artists carry enormous weight with their fans, and that our entire community is extremely brand-conscious. It's all about what you wear, what you drink, what you drive. It's not enough just to sing about a car, like the Beach Boys used to do. It's got to be a Cadillac or a Rolls or a Lexus. Diamonds might be a girl's best friend, like the old song says, but these days it's got to be a custom design piece from Icelink or Jacob the Jeweler, or something from Cartier or Rolex. We don't just drink champagne, it's Dom or Moet. Taken together, these product mentions seem to validate an artist, to signal that he or she has arrived, or to tele-graph to their audience what they're about. And from the fans' perspective, buying in to these trends is a way for them to emulate the artists who have become so important to their sense of self and community.

Most mainstream companies have been slow to appreciate the cause and effect. And some have rejected the attention. But there's no denying that something is going on here, and that this something is all tied up with our shared notion of who we are and how we live. Yeah, there's some shameless name-dropping out there. (Think Petey Pablo's "Freek-a-Leek": "Now I got to give a shout out to Seagram's gin/'Cause I'm drinkin' it and they payin' me for it.") But most of it comes from a lifetime of reaching up and out, and longing for the kind of success these name-brands symbolize.

We had about ten high-end shirts we tried to keep in circulation among these various artists, on video sets around the city. Wasn't just Hype Williams. We also hit up Diane Martel and any other music video director who would give us the time of day. You have to realize, most of the video shoots back then were out in the open. They were big deals, in our community. A lot of them were non-union jobs, with a lot of our friends from the neighborhood working as part of the crew. A lot of the artists were still on the way up, still living in the same community, still plugged in to the same crowd. Most times, one of us would know someone who knew someone who was involved. It was like six-degrees-of-separation, only it wasn't even that far removed. Usually, we were just once or twice removed from knowing someone like Hype Williams, or someone else high up on the set of each video, so there was always a way in. We'd find out where they were shooting, talk our way onto the set, hand out a shirt, wait around while they shot the video, take back the shirt, get it dry-cleaned, then find another set where we could hand out the same shirt all over again. In most cases, the artists and dancers were too happy to wear our clothes, because they were hot—and because we approached them with genuine respect. We were fans, first and foremost, and if we'd gone after these artists like it was a business deal, we probably wouldn't have gotten anywhere. These days, most product placement agents don't even know the artists' names, but we knew the lyrics to their songs. It meant something to us, you know.

We got a ton of publicity on the back of those first few shirts. The very first set we cracked in this way was a video shoot for "Punks Jump Up to Get Beat Down," by the group Brand Nubian. Jeff and Chaka set it up for us (they're the managers behind Ludacris's success), and that video ended up getting a ton of play, so we ended up getting a ton of play. We also got one of our shirts into a Mariah Carey video early on, with Old Dirty Bastard, and a video for "Where I Want to Be Boy," the second single for Miss Jones, which was about to break big.

Typically, there'd be about two months between the video shoot and the time these videos would start to get some airplay, so it took a while for us to see any results, and in the meantime we kept at it. Hard. There was another video in there for a group called Bitches With Attitude, another one of Hype's shoots. Sometimes we'd hang out at a set for ten, twelve hours and get nothing accomplished. I remember one long day on the set of a Grand Puba video, and we just couldn't get anyone to wear our clothes. Everybody was nice enough about it, and nobody seemed to mind that we were hanging around, but the look of our clothes didn't match up with the look of the video and we went home empty-handed—after eighteen hours of waiting around! That happened every once in a while, but we just kept hustling and hustling, lending out these ten shirts and maybe a couple hockey jerseys, and waiting for these videos to break.

Nowadays, this kind of stuff is often arranged beforehand, but in the early days of rap and hip-hop videos everything was a lot looser, a lot more casual. I even managed to jump into the shot myself, on a Biggie Smalls video. If you blink you might miss me, but if you look real fast you can catch me for half a second, popping in, wearing a FUBU hat.

When these videos started to break, our phone started to ring. In a big, relentless way. We were still a long way off from opening our own boutique, but a lot of small shops in and around New York City wanted to carry our line. All of a sudden, FUBU became the hot brand. There was a store called Montego Bay in Jamaica that was one of the first to give us some space, and another store out in the Green Acres Mall on Long Island. Our first prominent display at a Manhattan boutique was at a store called Bee's Knees, on Broadway, across from the downtown Tower Records. There was another store in the Bronx run by my boy Macho, and they also carried our clothes early on; their security guard was a no-name rapper who weighed just 170 pounds, who would go on to great fame (and great weight) as Big Pun. And for some reason, there were three or four stores out in Seattle, of all places, and another three or four in Japan, that started to carry our line. A lot of people look back at our launch and think we were made by these little stores in our black communities, but that's not how it happened. That was part of it, no question, but all kinds of people sparked to the FUBU line, and to the message behind it. Surfers and skateboarders were big for us, in the beginning, and we were happy to include everyone under our tent. Some of these stores only ordered twenty pieces, and we still had to figure out how to deal with the problem of consignment sales, but we figured it was worth the hassle. If they wanted to carry our clothes, we could find a way to make it work.

Clearly, these music video "product placements" became the cornerstone of our start-up operation. Already, we'd seen an enormous word-of-mouth type buzz through these Black Expos. People knew about our clothes and came looking for us. But that was purely regional. That was our grasp not quite exceeding our reach. These videos, though, put us on a whole other level, a national level, so I did a little quick research and came up with what I thought was an appropriate next move. I thought we'd head out to Vegas, to the Men's

Apparel Guild in California trade show, and try to make our first piece of real noise. It's a key show in the apparel business, the MAGIC show, and I knew we needed to be out there, that it was a logical next step, but that was about all I knew. I didn't know you needed to sign up as an exhibitor at least a couple weeks in advance in order to display your product on the trade show floor. I didn't know that we needed to dress for success and that our baggy jeans and loose t-shirts wouldn't quite cut it alongside all these turned-out fashion industry types.

I didn't even know that the clothing business ran on credit, that even if we wrote a whole bunch of orders all we'd have was a whole bunch of paper, promising payment on delivery. I might have known, considering the few stops and starts we'd had with some of those boutiques that worked on consignment, but it still hit me like a giant surprise. We'd still have to find a way to pay for the goods to hold up our end of the deal, and on top of that we'd still have to produce and deliver all those garments, and at some point on that first trip out to Vegas I caught myself thinking, That's a lot of hoops to jump through just to get paid.

>> GET THE BAGS, NORTON

Remember that old "Honeymooners" episode, where Ralph gets it in his head that he's about to be named in some old lady's will, and he and Norton go to the lawyer's office with an empty suitcase? The old lady had a parrot named Fortune, and every time the lawyer would read from the will where it said, "I bequeath my Fortune," Ralph would nudge Norton and tell him to get the bags ready.

Well, that was me, out in Vegas, expecting to catch a windfall of cash and to have to cart it back home to New York. I actually brought an extra suitcase on that first trip out to Vegas, thinking I'd need it to cart home the money we'd make writing all those orders. That's how I processed it. I just assumed we'd be rolling in cash. My partners looked at me like I was plain crazy, and I guess I was, but I'd seen too many television shows to know any better. Realize, it's not a metaphor, for me going out to Vegas with my hand out and my hopes up; it's the God's honest truth; I checked an extra bag, like I was some hapless hip-hop Ralph Kramden. I meant to pack it with bundles of cash. Like I said, I thought I was planning ahead. I thought I had everything covered. I even thought things through to where I imagined myself on the plane ride home, carrying the suitcase with me to the bathroom because I couldn't risk leaving it under my seat or in one of the overhead bins.

I look back on that first trip and it's almost embarrassing, me with my empty suitcase and all, but it's also funny. And instructive. It helps to remember that when you're just starting out you're bound to make some mistakes. You're bound to get a thing or two wrong, a time or two. It's like a rite of passage. You've got to screw up a little in order to get it right, and here we screwed up just enough.

It's the oldest line in business—*it takes money to make money*—but money was tight back then. Real tight. My pockets were like rabbit ears. There were five of us out there on this trip. My mother still had her job at American Airlines, so we were able to get out there for free, long as we flew stand-by. Naturally, we couldn't all head out there at once, because we couldn't count on there being enough stand-by seats to go around, so we staggered our itineraries. My partner Carl, he had a broken ankle, and it took him about 18 hours hanging at the terminal at JFK, just to get on a plane, and it turned out none of us were able to catch a flight directly to Vegas. We all flew to Los Angeles instead, and drove the rest of the way in a cheap rental car, but these were the resources available to us so we worked with what we had.

Once we got out to Vegas, we got ourselves a single hotel room at the Mirage, about five miles from the convention center where the MAGIC show was being held, and the accommodations were about as tight as our budget: one of us slept in the bathtub, two of us slept on the floor and the other two slept in the bed, head to toe. We quickly realized—of course—that our single hotel room would have to double as our showroom. Again, something we might have known going in, but we figured it out soon enough. We ran out to Home Depot, bought a clothing rack, put it up against the window and called ourselves designers. The room smelled like feet and fast food, and we only had seven or eight garments so there wasn't a whole lot for the buyers to look at once we got them up there (other than our own clothes, thrown about the place, our underwear sunnyside-up on the floor)—but, like I said, we didn't have the paper to do this first show up right.

>> WHAT THE MAGIC SHOW WOULD BECOME

That first MAGIC show, there were maybe one or two black designers on the floor. Today, there are a couple hundred—and a lot of industry types credit FUBU for the shift. (Or maybe they blame us, depending on their point of view.) Used to be your garden-variety trade show, but we started upping the ante each time out, and by now it's been transformed, in less than a decade. When we really took off, we started building bigger and bigger booths. We wanted people to wonder what we'd do next, to seek us out. One year, we put in a full basketball court—hardwood floors, fiberglass backboards—and brought in people like Magic Johnson to sign autographs. We threw elaborate parties, at places like the Rum Jungle, in Mandalay Bay. There were people hanging from trapezes, 300 models brought in from Los Angeles on chartered buses to help dress the room up a bit, open bar, open everything.

It got to where MAGIC became known as much for the party atmosphere as it was for apparel. It was almost like Fight Night in Vegas. You had people coming in to town just for the parties, young African-Americans making the scene, people who had nothing to do with the fashion industry.

Of course, now we tilt the other way. Now there's no reason for us to stand out like that. Now we're like the old grandfathers out at MAGIC. Now there are seven different parties every night, and there's nothing special about them. It's oversaturated, so we spend our money on other things, but each time I head out there I'm reminded how far we've come, how much has changed since that first trip.

Turned out the buyers didn't care about that smelly hotel room, or the five-mile haul from the convention center. Turned out there was enough heat around our line to get us past these few glitches. For all I know, our seat-of-the-pants *outsider* approach might have made us more attractive as designers. Clearly, we were out of our element, but that was the point of our entire line. It said as much right there on our label and in our logo: FUBU. *For us, by us.* We were a bunch of kids from Queens, taking our hustle out to Vegas to try to sell our goods to the big boys, so it made sense that we were cut a little differently. Our clothes were cut a little differently—and for good measure so were we.

Turned out, too, that we did a whole lot of things right. We'd gotten our t-shirts into enough music videos to create some vacuum, and some name recognition. We'd been featured on Ralph McDaniel's show back in New York, and placed an ad or two in the back pages of a couple magazines, so people were starting to know what we were about. We'd even gotten fellow Hollis native LL Cool J to wear our shirts and hats out in public, and to pose for a picture we were able to use in some print advertising. This right here is a story. LL had worn one of our red polar fleece jackets in this video he did with Boys II Men, for a song called "Hey Lover," and it got a ton of play. I sewed the thing myself, in my house, and I convinced him to wear it during the shoot. (Doesn't get more ground-floor than that!) I used to drive for LL's manager, Brian, and do a little work for him as a roadie. Once, I even drove home his dirty laundry to be cleaned. There might have been another dozen or so kids doing the same kind of thing, and most of them wanted to be rappers themselves, but I was drawn to the power of it. The proximity to all that money and fame . . . not to mention all those girls. And LL was cool about it. From when he got his first record deal, he was cool, and now he had a television show in the works, and he was starting to do movies, and he still came back to the neighborhood to check out his grandmother and keep connected. He remembered me well enough, and on one of these trips back home we got to talking. I told him what I was up to with my line of clothes, and he put it in my head to go after every person I could think of in the music business, from Russell Simmons on down, and get them into some type of FUBU product. The line he used (I'll never forget it) was that I should stalk them like a crazed pregnant woman. Be relentless, he said. Don't take no for an answer. Never let them breathe until they endorse you in some way.

So what did I do? I turned it back on LL—because, when it came down to it, he was the *only* person I really knew in the music business. I followed his advice and stalked *him* like a crazed pregnant woman. I learned from LL's new manager, Charles Fisher, that LL had to catch a plane one afternoon, so I grabbed a pile of clothes and a friend who knew how to work a camera and planted myself in front of LL's house, I guess on the thinking that it would be pretty hard for him to walk on by and not even stop to take a picture. Here again, I didn't know the first thing about endorsement deals, and of course it never occurred to me that if LL let himself be seen as a spokesperson for our little line of clothing he'd ace himself out of any potential deals with Levi's or Tommy Hilfiger or any other designer that might be in a position to actually pay him for the deal. We didn't have any money, and LL knew we didn't have any money, and I didn't realize it but I was putting him in a tough spot, hanging out in front of his house like that. But I kept at it, and eventually I wore him down. He had to come out to catch his plane at some point, and when he did I pressed it on him like the crazed, relentless pregnant woman he told me to be. Started slipping one of our shirts around his neck before he could shoo me away. LL was understandably irritated, and on serious edge, but then something clicked. He just shrugged, finally, in a *what the hell* kind of way, and said, "Alright, let's just take the shot."

LL posed with the group of us, and if you looked closely you could see my gold grills, that's how much of a street guy I still was at the time.

Anyway, my head nearly exploded, that's how much it meant, him throwing in and posing for us. Then he said, "If you ever get successful, you better not forget this."

And I haven't. Believe me, I haven't. And I never will. He might not see it the same way, but I will always be LL's biggest fan. For a while in there, he was our biggest fan as well. He even wore one of our hats in a GAP ad, and slipped in the phrase "For us, by us, on the low" in his rhyme. The ad ran nationally for weeks before GAP executives figured out the not-so-subliminal message, and it became a very famous example of guerilla marketing and a textbook case of David taking on Goliath, using Goliath's multi-million dollar ad budget without Goliath even knowing. Several heads from GAP and the responsible ad agency started to roll, and they pulled the campaign. However, it turned out that many African-Americans and hip-hop kids were coming into their stores looking for FUBU, and they ended up re-running those ads about a year later, because of the attention. There are only a handful of artists like LL in this regard—Fat Joe (the gatekeeper of the Latin market), Slim Thug, Bun B, Fabolous, Ja Rule, Rick Ross and Jay-Z—people who can go to the wall for you and your product, because they're not only artists, they're businessmen.

>> DISPLAY OF POWER

Knowledge is power.

Leverage is power.

Insight is power.

In the end, it all comes down to power, only here I'm not just talking about the power to buy and sell, or to hire and fire, or to beat on someone who does you dirt. After all, on some level, you start to think power is a kind of given. We expect it. We search for it in ourselves, and brace for it from our colleagues and competitors.

But if power itself is a given, where do we find our edge? These days, my take is that it's the display of power, above all. The appearance of power—and knowing what to do with it. It took that first trip to Vegas for this notion to register. Specifically, it took pulling up at a stop light in a cab driven by a guy who knew a thing or two about power. Those Vegas cabbies, man . . . they've seen everything. I was heading over to the convention center from my hotel. We pulled up alongside two antique Chevy sports coupes. Different colors, but the same model. One of the cars was being driven by a little old lady, just as polite as could be. The light turned green and you could see her ease gently back on the gas, but she was blocking traffic. And this other car was being driven by this young guy, looked to be about the same age as me, mid-twenties, and he was just cutting it up. Fishing-tailing, burning out, basically drag racing to each stoplight.

We caught up to the same two cars at the next light, and my philosophical cabbie turned back and said, "Look at that. Same two cars, but this one here, he's gonna get a display of power ticket?" He pointed to the car being driven by the young guy.

I said, "What?"

And the cabbie explained that this little old lady didn't have the slightest idea of the power she was sitting on, but this young kid was all full of adrenalin and ready to go. Same car, same engine, and this one's just a beast.

I'd never heard the phrase before—display of power—and that's when it hit me: two different people, all outward appearances they might look the same, but inside they just have no idea what they're capable of. Inside, they've got the same ability to turn it on and fire it up, but it's how we turn it on and fire it up that makes all the difference.

I've thought back to this exchange about a million times since that first Vegas trip, for the way it crystallizes the ways we set ourselves apart. We've all got the same package, more or less. We're all operating with the same machinery under the hood, the same engines. But it's what we do with those engines that determine whether we succeed or fail. It's how we strut that gives us our edge.

I ended up using that LL Cool J shot in a full-page ad in a magazine called *The Source*, and I ended up using tear-sheets of that ad as our promotional flier out in Vegas, and taken together it created the impression that we were a happening young company with a devoted following—not to mention the resources to hire a hip-hop icon like LL Cool J to endorse our line. Didn't really matter that we didn't have a booth on the convention floor. We had the *appearance* of a booth. We had the *display* of power and success. And so I'd hand out a flier and scrawl the name of our hotel and our room number on the back, and after a couple days we'd dragged enough major buyers through our tiny hotel room all the way across town from the trade show to account for nearly $400,000 worth of orders.

Four hundred thousand dollars!

You have to realize, that kind of money was incomprehensible to me at the time. Just off the charts, you know. And it wasn't just the money that set me reeling; what it represented was just so far off the map of my thinking that I couldn't begin to get my head around it. I was thrilled at the response the whole time we were in Vegas, but soon as I sat down on the plane headed home, I started to sweat. I started to obsess about the material I'd need to fill those orders. The machines I'd need to cut all those clothes. The workers I'd need to sew the product. The factory and warehouse space I'd need to set to work. And on and on. It got to where I looked around the cabin of that plane and caught myself thinking, What am I into here? But then I thought of my big, empty *Honeymooners* bag, stuffed into the over-head compartment above my head, and I realized full well what had gone on, what would happen next.

My suitcase may have still been empty, but we were finally in business—and good to go.

SMOKE

I flew back to New York, on my stand-by pass, and the main thought that kept bouncing around in my head was, *What the hell am I doing? What the hell am I doing? Whatthehellam-Idoing, whatthehellamIdoing, whatthehell . . . ?* Over and over and over. I had $400,000 worth of orders, but it was all just a mess of paper to me. Other than that, I had nothing. I couldn't think how to tap into those orders and turn them into revenue, how to put money in my pocket off the deal. How to make a *business* out of a hustle. Maybe that's because we were up all night partying before leaving Vegas, or maybe it's because I was in just a little bit over my head, but it was overwhelming to me, trying to figure how to fill all those orders—on time, at some type of profit. You might as well have slapped a scalpel in my palm and told me to perform brain surgery.

I was freaking out, a little bit. Overwhelmed. It took more than just money, even I knew that. It took knowledge and experience, education and maturity, only here too we came up a little short. What did I know about business? I worked at Red Lobster. I drove a livery van. If I earned a dollar, twenty-five cents would go to gas, and twenty-five cents would go to insurance. If I was going about it right, another twenty-five cents would get set aside for repairs and maintenance. The rest I could keep. But here I had to know about letters of credit, factors, giving terms to retailers, profit and loss statements, and like I said we came up a little short. Actually, we came up short on every last requirement or prerequisite except one, and here at last we had it covered: see, it also took balls to get a business like this off the ground, and on this one count, at least, me and my boys were packing.

Even so, for the first time since I thought about making this FUBU thing work, I started to think I was in over my head. I thought about quitting, and just leaving those orders hanging. I was intimidated by what lay ahead, and if somebody actually laid it out for me, what would happen next, what I'd have to go through to get to the next phase, I probably would have give up right there. But then I remembered a line I used to hear a lot: *The only goals you never achieve are the ones you never attempt.* So I thought, Okay, D, time to start attempting.

First order of business was to get some start-up money, so I could buy materials and hire people and start filling those orders. I'd already maxed out my credit cards (thank God for Amex), and been turned down for a loan at every banking and lending institution in the city. I'd jacked up my business plan and hit them all. Citibank, Greenpoint Bank, Chase, the Bank of New York . . . I knocked on every door. Still wasn't much of a business plan. It basically said, "Hey, give me *x* amount of dollars and if everything goes like we're hoping, I'll pay it back some day." It was one step removed from writing it all down on a napkin. And the response I received reflected that. I was turned down 27 times. I counted it up one day when I was feeling low, but the truth is I shouldn't have been surprised. I didn't know the first thing about banking or financing. I didn't know the first thing about writing an effective business plan. I didn't even know enough to wear a suit to these meetings. Nobody in their right mind should have loaned me money.

But I couldn't take "no" for an answer. For me, the word "no" is an absolute maybe.

Truth is, nobody should have loaned me money *before* the MAGIC show out in Vegas, but $400,000 worth of orders changed everything. All of a sudden, we were players. All of a sudden, we had something to trade. Anyway, that's how it seemed to me, how it should have gone, but it went another way. It went like this. The loan officer would say, "How much money do you actually have, Mr. John?" Or, "What are your assets?" And I'd say, "Actually, I'm thirty thousand dollars in debt." This wasn't what they wanted to hear, and I could tell this wasn't what they wanted to hear, so I'd usually add, "But our clothes are hot." To which they'd usually respond, "Well, can we see some of your samples?" "Ain't got no samples," I'd say, "but LL Cool J wears one of our shirts in his latest video." As if this might mean anything to these people, because of course they'd never heard of LL Cool J, so I would patiently explain that he was a popular rap artist, but then nine times out of ten these guys would have never heard of rap music either, so it was a little like trying to sell a bag of weed to a priest. I was speaking a completely different language.

>> NEW MONEY

Most people were slow to recognize the purchasing power of the black community. Specifically, most mainstream white people were slow to recognize it, which is why none of these banker-types could spot an opportunity here. The thinking was, why reach out to a market that had never really contributed to any bottom line?

Truth was, there was money to be made, because all of a sudden there was money to be spent, and if I was smart enough to write a halfway decent business plan I might have shown how FUBU could tap into that. I'll explain: early 80s or so, you started to see a new stream of money flow into our urban neighborhoods. It used to be that the streets were run by older black gentlemen, pimps and dope dealers and numbers runners. If you'd somehow managed to make it to middle age, you'd earned a place of respect, just by virtue of the fact that you weren't in jail or in the ground. Now, though, there were other paths to success for young black people—legitimate paths to suc- cess—and all these young guys had blown by their elders, in all areas. Remember, we were the first generation to grow up in the post civil rights era, and the benefits of that struggle had filtered down. Music, sports, education, business . . . there was opportunity all around. Real opportunity.

Okay, so that was one factor. The other factor was that there was also a new drug on the street, crack cocaine, and it changed everything. Crack wasn't the high-end cocaine being sold at clubs like Studio 54. It was a cheap, five-dollar high, and it turned our world upside down—on the user end and the dealer end, both. All of a sudden you had young rappers hitting it big overnight, and superstar ath- letes throwing their money around like it was noth- ing at all, and underneath all of that were these young black kids getting easy-money rich selling crack, parroting the culture of excess exhibited by their favorite rappers and athletes, buying into the same ideal. It all kind of fed into each other.

There was a real shift in the urban black community, by the mid-80s, to where everything started to skew young and aggressive and in-your-face. Bling became the currency of choice. Young blacks started to spend money like they'd never had any before, like they'd never see this type of money again. Wearing what you hustled on your wrist, or around your neck . . . that became the way of the street. No one thought about saving any money, or investing, because no one expected to be around long enough to spend through their bankroll. It was easy-come, easy-go, and while you had it the thing to do was let your money do your talking. Kanye West talks about it in one of his songs, how we quickly became the first group to buy our pride and wear it on our sleeves, and he had it dead-on.

As a consumer group, African-Americans went from having no disposable income to having only disposable income in the time it took to check out a new club, and in the shakeout there were start-up companies like Walker Wear, Def Jam, Bad Boy, Death Row, 40 Acres and a Mule, Karl Kani and now FUBU, looking to make some noise on the back of this cultural shift. Ten years earlier, we could never have sold a refashioned hockey jersey for a hundred bucks—but now that was only a place to start.

Turned out the way I had to play it was to take out a second mortgage on the house on Farmers Boulevard. Wasn't exactly the smartest move in the world, but I was going on balls. I borrowed another $100,000 against the house, and used it to buy ten industrial sewing machines, and enough material to fill the first batch of orders. Then I turned over about half the house and it made it into a factory. My girlfriend at the time, she ended up being my wife and the mother of my children, she went out and found a half-dozen or so Latino women for me to sew the product. (None of them spoke any English, but they were good workers.) The house had about 3,500 square feet, and the only spaces we didn't utilize for the business were the attic, one of the bedrooms, the kitchen, and a little bit of the basement. Every other square inch of space, we put to some kind of FUBU use. I put a huge table in the dining room, and used it to cut fabric. I met a guy named Greg, a real West Indian sewer, and he knew how to cut patterns, so I put him in charge of cutting our garments. He parked himself in the dining room, and went to work on that giant table. I made an office for me and my boys in one of the rooms upstairs, and we all made it a point to be there whenever our schedules allowed.

In all, those $400,000 worth of orders represented about 15,000 garments, so that was a ton of fabric and a ton of activity. Giant rolls of fabric filled up the living room and the rest of the basement. People were constantly coming and going. There were four or five of us living there and another ten or so working there. We worked all hours. There were deliveries all day. Some mornings, our dutiful band of Latino sewers would report for work and have to bang on the door for a while, or shout up at an open window before one of us could get out of bed and open for business. In the winter they'd huddle outside my front door and shout, "Frio!" and I'd look out the window and see their red noses.

From the frantic, random way we ran the place, it might have been a sweatshop in lower Manhattan, and I'm sure my neighbors must have scratched their heads over all the noise. Some of them were probably pretty pissed, because outside of me and my boys, it was basically a quiet, residential neighborhood. We weren't zoned for any kind of commercial or industrial use, but we went at it like we needed to in order to get the job done. And it was a nice-enough neighborhood. It's not like there were all these burnt-out buildings doubling as crack-houses. There were honest, hard-working people, up and down the street. Families. And yet we basically ran that place like a factory, at all hours, with little or no regard for our neighbors, and after just a couple days our excess materials started to pile up and we needed to figure out what to do with it. We didn't have the money to get a dumpster and dispose of the stuff properly.

So I took the easy way out and burned it. I'd seen all those bums, burning tires to keep warm in the winter, so I thought we could do the same, which was probably a fool move because we were burning polar fleece and other synthetic materials. Yeah, I know, it was absolutely illegal, but that didn't stop us. We had a huge empty oil drum set up in the back of the house, and there'd be this toxic purple cloud hanging over the entire neighborhood. We weren't exactly inconspicuous—I'll say that. The fire department would come out to the house every week, just about. They'd kick down the door and hose down the yard. We'd hear the sirens and take that as our signal to hop the fence and run to the Chinese spot where we'd stand outside drinking 40's for a couple hours until the trouble passed. Then we'd come back a couple hours later and there'd be a ticket on the front door. It's like we were still back in high school, retooling our hot cars, looking over our shoulders to make sure we weren't caught—and yet at the other end we were scrambling to fill orders for established retail outlets, for businessmen who had a right to expect that their goods were being manufactured by legitimate means.

We were working crazy, relentless hours, and the pressure we put on ourselves to meet these orders was also pretty crazy, but we kept at it. There's another line that kept bouncing around my head around this time: *Sacrifice is giving up something of lesser value for something of greater value.* Couldn't say for sure what that something of greater value would turn out to be, but we could certainly give up our free time and our sanity for the next while and see what it got us.

Our initial orders from that first MAGIC show called for four basic items, in various sizes and quantities: a polar fleece sweat suit, pants and top; a sweatshirt; and an embroidered scuba-type jacket, made out of some neoprene-type material. Busta Rhymes ended up wearing one of those scuba jackets in one of his first big videos, so it became a hot item for us. In addition to those four items, there were another six or so that we would buy as blanks and hook up with our own logo—t-shirts, hats, that sort of thing. Wasn't much of a line—but hell, wasn't much of an operation, either. At least not yet.

>> LOOK THE PART

I spent a disproportionate amount of time designing our first hang tag, because I thought the look would say a lot about our line. A hang tag, I'd quickly learned, is the tag that hangs from a new garment. (For a guy who didn't know a thing, I figured this one out pretty quick.) I wanted to do it up right. With a new clothing line, a lot of times it's something simple like a hang tag, something that doesn't have anything to do with the garment itself, that stamps you and sets you apart. It could be a logo, or an iconic image of some kind, or a memorable slogan, like the "Nothing comes between me and my Calvins" line delivered so famously by Brooke Shields, so many years earlier.

You never know what will catch on and make some noise for you. I'd admired the hang tags of designers like Karl Kani, and I figured there must be other idiots out there just like me who paid a little too much attention to this type of thing, so I put my energy into this one area. I used to catch myself looking at Karl Kani's picture on his hang tags before we even got FUBU up and going, and I'd think, Well, if he can do it, then so can I.

We already had the memorable slogan—"For Us, By Us"—so it made sense to cover as much ground as possible, to reinforce the brand in every way available to us. I saw it as free follow-up advertising. We'd make our sale, and the customer would take the garment home, and there'd be this great hang tag laying around, leading them to their next purchase.

We had a nice shot taken of the four of us—me, Keith, J and Carl—and we looked like a bunch of rappers from Queens. Rappers, thugs, whatever . . . I thought it really sold what we were about, and would help to make our brand identifiable in the marketplace. Plus, it put a face to our line—four faces, actually—which I thought couldn't hurt as we were looking to establish ourselves. All these other designers on their hang-tags, they were white, and flamboyant, and vaguely European. I liked that we all had a different look about us, a different attitude. Keith was a little grimy. Carl was smooth. J was slick. And me, I was clean-cut. Together, we had it covered, and in the back of my head I was thinking that in success we could each become associated with the FUBU brand. There'd be four faces of FUBU, and we could spread ourselves around, and wherever we'd go, to different clubs, to different concerts, someone could point to any one of us and say, "Hey, that's the FUBU guy!"

So that's what we went with on the tag, and we took a little heat for it in some circles. It's like we were stars in our own right, the way the four of us were posing on those tags, where in reality we weren't even stars in our own minds. We were still scrambling to fill our first orders, still operating out of my house on Farmer's Boulevard, still working our other full-time jobs, still running like hell whenever the cops or the fire department came to the door because we knew were in violation of . . . something. But we looked like designers, that was the key. We looked like we cared about what we were doing, what we were selling, what we were hoping to build with this small piece of momentum, and as we started to fill those first few orders and hang these tags from our first "official" items, I realized how important it was for us to look the part. You know, to give the appearance that we were on top of our game, that we knew what we were doing. Perception becomes reality.

Appearance, I realized, is key, even in a small detail such as this, because we went from being a bunch of guys working tirelessly behind the scenes to get their clothing line off the ground, to a bunch of guys out in front, representing. I didn't plan on it, but it turned out our customers would buy a shirt and feel like they had helped us out, like they had done us some sort of solid. Turned out, too, that this wasn't such a bad way to build a brand—and some all-important customer loyalty.

The garbage was a real concern. There was a lot of excess fabric. Once we figured out what we were doing, we'd learn to cut the fabric in such a way that we'd minimize the excess, but back then there was a lot of waste. Also, we'd get a lot of our shipments from overseas in big wooden crates, or the fabric would be wound around these enormous heavy-cardboard poles, and those would all be lying around, cluttering up the house and the yard. The garage was jammed with all the furniture and carpets we had to take from the house, but there was a ton of stuff we couldn't fit in there. My mother was a real pack rat. She grew up poor, so she couldn't throw anything away. Plus, my father had built the house, and all his building materials were still there. Nails, plastic, fiberglass, BX cable . . . and I had to get rid of it all to make room for our operation.

It all piled up to where I used to spend a couple hours each night in the yard out back, burning everything, and I spent so much time facing that big oil drum, with those big, roaring flames, I turned about four shades blacker on one side of my body. If I'd known you could get a fireburn like that, standing so close to the flames, I would have turned around every once in a while, gotten an even tan. My hair started falling out a little bit on that one side, and my skin was constantly hot. The occupational hazard to end all occupational hazards.

Even the grass in the backyard started to develop these little burnt-out circles, from wherever the drum would be, so from on high it looked like these weird urban crop patterns left by some UFO.

Some nights, we'd make it a party. My neighbors would look out the window and see four or five young black guys with their shirts off, standing around a burning oil drum, drinking 40-ounce bottles of beer. Once in a while, someone would yell down to us to keep it quiet, and we'd say, "Get back in your house, old lady," or whatever. These poor people—we were their worst nightmare. They were living in hell. I feel bad for them now, I really do, but back then I was too arrogant and focused to give them a thought. We had our own crap we had to slog through, same as them.

And the thing of it is, we had no idea if this clothing line would actually work. It *felt* like our ticket up and out, but you never know. The four of us were at it so hard, in such close quarters, sleeping maybe three hours a night, that at least one of us talked about quitting every week or so. There was tension and stress and occasional fist fights when our tempers ran away from us. But at the end of each day we were brothers, fighting the good fight, in on the same deal. Yeah, it was just a bet, but we all felt it was a good bet. We were still making our money on the come, running around like crazy, trying to fill these first orders, making some of the local deliveries ourselves to cut down on shipping costs, grabbing a couple hours sleep here and there. It's like we were all living in a strange bubble, underneath that strange purple cloud hovering over my house. We worked our day jobs, we worked our FUBU sideline, we networked at clubs and parties and music video sets . . . and we waited to hit it big. We counted on it.

The trick came in seeing it coming. In those days, we still had a little black and white television in the house, no cable, and I had it set up in the kitchen. One of those rabbit-eared sets, with the tin foil on the antenna. We'd see one of our videos come on Ralph McDaniels' show and get all excited. First couple times it happened, we were jumping all around, clapping each other on the back, just out of our minds. Then we got used to it, but it never completely lost that little thrill. I still get amped every time I see one of my garments on a rap artist or celebrity. I get an even bigger charge when I see someone wearing one of our shirts out on the street or in a club, because that to me is just about the ultimate validation of what we do. But those first few times, seeing one of our hockey jerseys or jackets or t-shirts in a video . . . that was big-time, and we just hoped like hell the second-mortgage money held out long enough for us to fill all our orders.

>> 05

Wasn't long before every company on the planet began to target music videos as a promotional tool. I'm surprised it took that long, but by the butt-end of 1995, front-end of 1996, after we had about a six-month running start, MTV began blurring the logos and images on videos that seemed to be a little too strategically placed on and around the artists who appeared in their featured videos. I guess their thinking was, if Pepsi or Ralph Lauren or Mercedes-Benz was going to advertise on their network, they were going to pay for it, which meant that even if we convinced an artist to wear our clothes the FUBU logo would be scrambled.

Still, a music video in heavy rotation on MTV was worth millions, in terms of product placement and brand recognition. All those repeat plays . . . it was like buying a 30-second spot on the Super Bowl. No way was I gonna let those suits at MTV close this little backdoor on me without some kind of fight. I knew there had to be a way around the MTV censors—there's always a way!—and I came up with a new logo that I thought would be scramble-proof and at the same time signal our brand. I stole the idea from a lot of clothing companies, like Abercrombie & Fitch and Polo, which used the year of their launch in a lot of their designs, and Nike, which used Michael Jordan's uniform number, 23, as a kind of brand, only in our case I wasn't out to celebrate any anniversary or sports icon. I was out to celebrate me and my partners, and since there were five of us (me, Keith, Carl, J and that fifth Beatle), I hit on the number 05. For a while in there, we put that number on everything. Shirts, jackets, hockey jerseys, hats . . . To most people, it just looked like a number on a team uniform, but of course no athlete wore a 0 in front of the 5. He just wore number 5, so we were somewhat unique. Plus, we were still a couple years from Y2K, so the year '05 wasn't even on people's radar, let alone embroidered on their clothes, which meant we had that number pretty much to ourselves. (And, thinking like my boy Prince, I knew that if FUBU made it to 2005 there'd be a nice pay-off, in brand-awareness terms.)

We put that 05 on almost every item we made, for a time, and after a while people began to associate it with the FUBU line. We didn't have to spell it out for everyone; people just knew, same way they knew what our name stood for, even though we'd never spelled that out for people after that first run of shirts. We even went out and registered the number for this type of use, and a couple years later we won a $6 million lawsuit against another company that tried to infringe on our trademark.

The point, though, is not that it pays to CYA with lawyers and trademarks (although it certainly helps), but to keep thinking outside the box, and recognizing that the box keeps moving, and changing shape. Music videos had been our way in to this market, and very quickly the rules of the game changed on us so we had to shift gears. Not a whole lot, but just enough to stay out in front. Busta Rhymes wearing one of our scuba jackets was priceless—but priceless could shoot to worthless in no time at all if our logo was blurred and people at home couldn't make the FUBU connection. The 05 was the FUBU connection. It symbolized the four of us in on this pipedream, and it left room for that fifth open spot, for the partner who never managed to stick. And it kept us in the game.

At some point, in the middle of all this craziness and excitement and busting-our-asses, my mother pulled me aside and told me I was out of my mind. I think those might have been her exact words. She didn't like to interfere, but she pressed it. Told me I was an idiot for trying to finance this thing myself. I tried to explain that the banks wanted no part of our business, but she wasn't hearing it. She said,

"Daymond, you've got to use other people's money. That's the only way to make it in this world." She felt so strongly about it, she took out a classified ad in the Sunday New York Times, without even telling me. The ad said something like, "One million dollars in orders, need financing." And we got a couple dozen calls on it. By the next day, a Monday, our answering machine was full. About half the calls were vague inquiries, from people wanting to know a little bit more about our situation, what kind of business we were in, what the orders represented, that sort of thing. Another ten were from mobsters and loan-shark types, guys with names like Sal, Vinnie or Bareback Louie wanting to shake me down, offering outrageous terms, like fifty percent. One or two of them wanted pictures of my family to secure the deal, so there was no way I was doing business with these characters.

But three or four of the calls were from legitimate garmentos, fashion industry executives on the prowl for a good investment opportunity, so I set up some meetings. I'd take my mother, and I realize now what a strange picture I must have made, this street kid from Hollis, taking his mother with him to a straight-up business meeting. But my mother knew her stuff. These guys would look at me like I was some mama's boy, but I didn't care. Dee and Wah of Ruff Ryders used to bring their pops with them to meetings, and he was a respected guy and nobody gave them any grief for it. This was my version of the same thing. My mother had my back; she was my dog. She knew what questions to ask, what questions we'd need to take back to our lawyer after each meeting. And she was a good judge of people.

In one of those meetings, we sat down with Norman Weisfeld, from Samsung's textile division, and his brother Bruce, who was running the family business, who would go on to become my partners and good friends. We didn't get off to the best start, though. I met with them at their offices in the Empire State Building, and they seemed interested in doing a deal with us. Their main business was bubble coats, which mean things were slow six months out of the year, when the rest of the business was selling summer. They were looking to expand. Unfortunately, me and my "posse" didn't make the strongest first impression, and for years these guys would razz me about being the asshole who brought his mother with him to do a deal, but it didn't bother me. They were right. It must have been pretty funny, to sit across the table from me and my mother, but that was my comfort zone. I liked having her at my side, and I was smart enough to recognize that sometimes it's the people closest to you who have the most to offer, in terms of wisdom and insight and experience.

First time we met, a couple months after that first MAGIC show, Norman and Samsung were also looking to do a distribution deal with another designer named Benny Miles—*Sir* Benny Miles, actually. That's what he called himself. I somehow found out that Sir Benny himself was sitting in the next room, while I was meeting with Norman and Bruce, and I took it as a giant show of disrespect. I mean, I could certainly understand Benny's right to pursue the same kind of deal we were after. And I could understand that these guys might have been talking to any number of young designers, and that they would probably wind up only doing one of these deals, but to play one designer off the other, with one tucked away in a back room like that . . . it set me off.

To Benny's credit, he knew how to sew. Technically, he could design me and my partners under the table. He could do a suit. He could do a bubble coat. He could do a pair of pants. Put him in a room for a half-hour and he'd come out with the best-looking coat you'd ever want to see. He was super-talented. But the world is full of talented people who are technically proficient but lack the drive or the instincts or the contacts to make a meaningful impact. Benny didn't have $400,000 worth of orders, or access to artists like Mariah Carey and Busta Rhymes. He couldn't get LL Cool J to wear his

product, or get his clothes into the clubs. He couldn't connect the power of music with the power of persuasion, the power to remind people of times, places, smells, colors, styles, and the fact that music packs such an emotional charge that if you find a way to connect it to the consumer market you'll be so far ahead of your competitors they couldn't even find you with a map. It's the soundtrack to our lives, and we had a bead on it that guys like Sir Benny couldn't match. So, clearly, we brought different things to the table, and Norman and Bruce and them had to decide whether they wanted someone with pure, technical skills, or these four, raw street guys who were somehow plugged in to the Rap and Hip-Hop community. It was a tough call, even I could see that, but I didn't like that they had Benny in the other room while we had our meeting. That, to me, was a deal-breaker—if there was even a deal to be made. There weren't any terms on the table just yet, but I was ready to walk over something like this. Fortunately, though, I kept my cool, and I kept my mouth shut. My mother kept telling me we would never get the best deal based on what I would ask for, but on what I could negotiate. That basically meant I had to sit back and seethe until these guys made an offer. Then I could toss it back to them and lay out my own terms.

Meanwhile, they kept stringing Benny along, and they kept stringing us along, and for all I knew they were stringing a couple other designers along as well. They even had Benny doing some work for them, on some kind of retainer, while we kept scrambling to fill our orders. Like I said, some stores were paying us C.O.D., but some were taking 90 days to make payment, so our second-mortgage money was depleting. There was some money coming in, but not enough to keep ahead of the money going out, and I was too stupid to realize that we were desperate to do a deal. We *needed* Norman and Bruce, but I didn't know that.

Finally, Norman called with an offer: they would cover all our costs and front us the money we'd need to develop our line, in exchange for two-thirds of our business. I've since learned that this was pretty much the standard deal in the garment industry, for a backer looking to come in and handle the financing and the distribution, but all I cared about was that we'd be *covered*. There'd be nice salaries for me and my boys. Nice offices. We could leave our other jobs and throw in full-time on this FUBU push. We'd be set.

>> NEGOTIATING FROM IGNORANCE

Here's a business strategy you won't find anywhere else: approach every deal like you don't have a clue or a care in the world. Come to every negotiating table uninformed and unprepared. Treat every deal point as an affront. Be prepared to walk over the smallest thing.

Look, the conventional wisdom is you're supposed to negotiate from strength. That's where you find your best deal. But our strength at FUBU was also our weakness. We were street-wise, with a hard-won street ethic that pretty much flew in the face of most boardroom exchanges. We were raw and unsophisticated. I didn't know the first thing about how to handle myself in a bona-fide business negotiation. I wasn't patient or subtle or charming.

And yet in my case ignorance was bliss, because if I'd known half of what I needed to know in order to get FUBU off the ground, I wouldn't have even bothered trying. If I'd seen all the hurdles, I'd have looked elsewhere. And if I had any sort of poise or polish to me I wouldn't have been the arrogant guy who attracted potential investors to our business in the first place. Yeah, we were the hottest line out there, by the time we got to Norman and Bruce Weisfeld. Yeah, we had all these orders, and the promise of a lot more. Yeah, there was more buzz around us than you'd find in a honey factory. But we were almost down to our last dollar. We had no real business sense, no formal schooling. And we had no business not accepting a standard distribution deal like the one being offered.

The Las Vegas MAGIC show was a twice-yearly event, and there was another one coming around on the calendar, but I couldn't get Norman on the phone to accept his deal. I kept calling and calling. Meanwhile, I had no real idea what was happening on the other side of the table. Turned out Norman and Bruce had been having a difficult time making a go of it. Business was tough. Their father had started the family business. He was a Holocaust survivor. He always instilled in them to keep the doors open, no matter what. He used to talk about how you never knew who was going to walk through those doors. Their father was an extremely strong man. I guess you'd have to be, to survive the Holocaust. And Bruce religiously kept that philosophy, so they were just hanging in there, trying to get something going. If their father knew they were keeping the doors open so that four black kids from Queens could walk through it, he might have thrown up his hands and shouted *Oy vey!* But to their great credit, that's just what they were doing, only they weren't doing it fast enough for us to take advantage of the upcoming MAGIC show.

Without a deal, then, I figured we could head out to Vegas and find another investor, on the back of all the heat that was still attached to our line. And so, next thing we knew me and my boys were again out in Vegas, again on our American Airlines passes, again on the cheap. We didn't even bother to bring out a new line to sell, because we still had that mess of orders to fill. If we took in any more business, it might have derailed the whole operation. Our agenda this time out was to scare up some other potential investors, so we walked the floor of that convention center in our FUBU threads, hoping to attract some attention. And, sure enough, we did. Wasn't the kind of attention we were after—meaning, no one came forward and offered us a deal—but people noticed us, that's for sure. We handed out the same tear sheets we used that first MAGIC show, the ones with LL Cool J. I remember walking by the Lugz booth, where a buyer from Dr. Jay's was hanging with about 25 other retailers, and the guy hollered out at us and said, "Man, you guys have got the hottest line on the street, period. Where can I find you?"

It was good to hear, and it just so happened that Norman and Bruce had a booth right next to Lugz. Bruce overheard everything. I couldn't have set the whole thing up any sweeter. So that put the whole thing in motion all over again. Bruce got on the phone to Norman right away and said, "Whatever happened to that FUBU deal? These guys are hot as hell. We better do this deal. Now."

It was just a chance comment that Bruce Weisfeld happened to overhear, but I have to think it would have gotten back to him and his brother one way or another. We were definitely in play, and the center of some serious attention. We were like a shared secret, and everybody wants in on a secret, right? Plus, it's a relatively small business. Everyone knows everyone else. And every season, it seems, there's a new line that comes out of the MAGIC show with all the excitement and attention, and even though we weren't exhibitors we were the flavor of the moment. Somehow or other, we would have come once again to Norman and Bruce's attention, and they would be reminded of the deal that seemed to have gotten away from them.

Norman called, soon as I got back to New York, but I wouldn't take his first call. Wouldn't take his second or third calls, either. I was still a little rough around the edges, still a little unsure how this pride and respect thing might play in big-time Corporate America, but I didn't like the way this guy treated me that first time around. Yeah, he made us a fair offer, but I didn't like that he'd left us hanging, all that time. He didn't return my phone calls, so I wouldn't return his, and when he did finally get me on the line I told him he was full of it.

"What do you mean?" he said. "I want to do a deal."

I told him again that he was full of it. Then I think I hung up on him. I was nasty as hell, and to this day I'm not sure why. It was just business, at that point, and looking back Norman hadn't really done anything but keep his options open and refuse to give away the store, but for some reason I took it personal. For some reason it felt like he kept me dangling, on that first pass. And it's not like I had any other deals to fall back on. We did turn up a couple other would-be investors on that trip out to Vegas for our second MAGIC show, but I didn't like those deals either, so we were no closer to any kind of long-term solution.

The thing of it is, I didn't think I *needed* to do a deal with anyone at that point. I thought I was rich. I was filling my orders, and I had every reason to believe there'd be more orders on the back of that first batch. Our shirts and jackets were in heavy rotation in various music videos. We were "hot," whatever that meant. But I was too dumb to look even just a couple months into the future and make a realistic assessment of our prospects. Truth was, in two more months, I would have been bankrupt. Four months, I probably would have had to sell the house.

But Norman was persistent. He kept after me, and he wore me down, and this time he came back with an even better deal, probably better than one I could have negotiated for myself. Me and my boys got to keep FUBU for ourselves. At Norman's suggestion, we would keep full control and ownership of our brand and our trademark. He wasn't just being generous. He was smart enough to realize that this type of set-up would carry enormous benefits in the black community, where being black-owned and operated can really distinguish your brand. It would be good for us, good for business—and, ultimately, good for Norman and Bruce. So that's the way we played it, and then on top of FUBU we formed a holding company, which we split down the middle, and we slotted FUBU into that, so at the end of the day I could look myself in the mirror and know we'd taken care of business. *Our* business.

Norman had this one right. Absolutely, in the black community it's a great big deal to be able to point to a black company and know that it's genuinely black-owned. It's like a street version of the *Good Housekeeping* seal of approval. It means you can be trusted, and supported, and pointed to with pride. It means you're authentic. Yeah, in one respect we were partnering up with these nice Jewish boys from Samsung, fifty-fifty, but if they ever failed to hold up their end of the deal we'd still own FUBU outright. We'd still be the public face of our company. We'd still keep true to ourselves, and to the credo behind our name: *for us, by us.*

>> YOUNG, GIFTED AND BLACK-OWNED

Along with that shift in the purchasing power of the black community came a sense or responsibility to keep that money within the black community, wherever possible. The line you started to hear was, "Yeah, you're making all this money, but you're spending it with the white man." And underneath that line was the caution that we had to take care of our own, and an unspoken pressure on each of us to do our part.

Let's face it, in a city like New York, we didn't have to look far to see examples of other minority groups taking care to fuel their own community. The Chinese did a great job of re-circulating their money, buying Chinese goods and services, from Chinese merchants. The Italians, in neighborhoods like Little Italy, were able to do the same. But in the black community, it was unusual to find a sense of supporting each other, of a rising tide lifting all boats—in part because there had only been a small community of black business leaders and manufacturers in need of our support.

In my own household, growing up, this had never been an issue. My mother would go to the white neighborhoods to buy better cuts of meat from the white butcher. I'd go to Macy's to buy Polo, or Louis Vuitton, or Timberlands . . . whatever was hot. You know, there weren't a whole lot of black merchants to begin with, but what few there were, we took the attitude, If we get to them, we get to them.

And yet that all started to change, around the time of the Rodney King riots, around the time all this new money started to flow into our community. The new thinking seemed to be, now that the money had finally found us, we'd do well to keep it near. To be "black-owned" became a point of honor, the same way mainstream Americans once pointed with national pride to clothes or cars or computers that were "Made in the U.S.A." To spend your money at a "black-owned" business was doing your part. It was almost expected. It became such a big deal in the black community during the rioting that Chinese and Latino merchants would spray-paint the words "black-owned" on their windows, hoping the thugs and vandals would do the right thing and pass them by.

It was the kind of thinking that laid the foundation for FUBU, and it was one of our principal assets—our calling card. And I wasn't about to trade it for the world.

It was a good deal all around. We got our pay-day, and a little bit of breathing room in filling these pending orders, and a show of respect we took as key. And the Weisfelds, with Samsung's backing, got a partnership with a "hot" brand and access to our various contacts in the rap and hip-hop communities. We went to work right away. The very next day, after we signed the papers, we started going to our new offices in the Empire State Building and ramping down our factory operation in the house on Farmers Boulevard. Wasn't exactly room for all of us in those offices, but we fit ourselves in—I guess on the thinking that we'd better make ourselves at home before Norman and Bruce and them could change their minds.

There was about a three-month turnaround, as we moved our manufacturing to the Samsung side, and as we helped transition our new partners from an outerwear company to a sportswear company. Their family business had been bubble coats, and that's what they knew; they needed to learn how to make jeans and t-shirts and sweatshirts; they needed to understand our market. One of our first priorities was to get ourselves in line with the seasons, meaning that we started shipping our heavier winter goods early, so that they'd be in stores for the winter selling season, instead of whenever the hell we got around to filling the order, which is how we'd been going about our business. That kind of half-assed approach was fine, for a rag-tag bunch of upstarts from the 'hood, and we could have probably gotten away with it for another season or two, but it was time to get our act together and plan for some kind of future. Our future.

We'd do it up right, or not at all.

FIRE

Empire State Building, 48th floor. That's where we landed. On one level, it might have felt like we'd arrived, but I don't think we looked on it as hitting the big time just yet. I guess you could say we were like King Kong—a big beast climbing its way to the observation deck, scaring the natives in our path, but we still had a way to go. There was a lot of work ahead of us, a lot that had to fall our way, and we'd all seen our boys from the neighborhood flame through more money than we were making in a single drug deal.

Anyway, if this wasn't the big time it was close. We were riding the elevators each day in a serious landmark building, with people in serious suits out to make some serious cash. And guess what? We were holding our heads high and holding our own. With our salaries we were making enough to bounce from Farmers Boulevard and into places of our own—not right away, mind you, but we each had a foot out the door when we signed the distribution deal. I drew an initial salary of about $50,000. Carl and J drew slightly less. Keith didn't sign on just yet—he was still working in building management, still not sure we could make a go on this FUBU deal—but we kept on him about making a decision, and it took a couple weeks until he eventually threw in, and at that point we were finally good to go.

The primary obligation to Samsung was to keep doing what we were doing—and to ship at least $5 million worth of product in the first three years or the deal was off. Don't know how we came up with that number or that timetable, but it seemed like a reachable goal, given the orders we managed to book on that one Vegas trip and the ones that trickled in through our limited advertising. Turned out it took only four or five months to meet our target, and I look back now and think it had to do with the vision we had for our clothes. We struck a kind of chord. Yeah, the high-profile push we continued to get from rap and hip-hop artists kept us out in front and in the mix, but it was more than that. And it was more than the simple fact that we wanted to make our own clothes and call our own shots. It was that we had a clear concept in mind, and that no other company was taking the same approach. We knew what we liked to wear, how hard it was to find, and how much we could justify spending. We weren't out to reinvent the wheel, but we were hoping to spin it in a fresh new way.

>> DRESS FOR SUCCESS

Before FUBU, we were buying Carhartt and Timberland and North Face—technical, performance-based gear. No good reason except we liked the way the stuff looked. No question, it was overkill, far as we were concerned. It was like wearing top-of-the-line scuba gear to wade in a kiddie pool. I mean, Carhartt makes clothes for construction workers, using flame-resistant fabrics, and Timberland makes rugged outdoor gear, filled with Gor-Tex and fiberglass and all that . . . and we only bought it for the design. We didn't need to spend $800 on a ski jacket. We didn't care if it kept us warm in sub-zero temperatures, or if it had pockets for our ski goggles. We just wanted to wear this stuff while we stroked the streets of our neighborhood.

That's the mindset we took to our first line. We could cut out all these bells and whistles and performance elements and retail a nice coat for three hundred dollars, which opened up a whole new market. The design was still there, but we'd take out the technical stuff and focus on the stuff the 'hood cared about. Our bells and whistles were stash pockets—because, hey, you could never have enough places to stow your cell, or your condoms, or your weed.

Style, comfort, affordability . . . that's what we looked for in our designs. We also looked at what some of our counterparts were doing and tried to play off of that. If Nike came out with a Carolina blue sneaker with a burnt orange swoosh, for example, we'd make a Carolina blue shirt with a burnt orange FB on it. We were big into footwear, me and my boys, so we tried to get a little ensemble thing going in that area, to make sure our customers didn't have to go to Nike or Adidas or some other company to coordinate their look with their sneakers. They could come to us.

Quality was key. If you bought one of our sweat-shirts, it would be made from the heaviest mate-rial we could find. It would be embroidered, not screen-printed, and the appliqué would be as thick as possible. The zippers would have some weight and last to them. The garment wouldn't shrink. It wouldn't nap up. Nice. And the dyes we used would be as wet as we could manage without running, because that's what gave you those rich, vibrant colors. You know, a lot of the sweatshirts and t-shirts that were out at the time used to have a dis-tressed or faded look to them. That was a certain style. But in urban fashion, you wanted your clothes to look as new and fresh as possible. You wanted those colors to pop, and really announce who you were and what you were about. That faded, raggedy look was for rich white kids looking to dress down in their worn-out designer clothes. We rolled another way.

The big trend in urban fashion in the mid '90s was towards clothes that were a little bigger and baggier than a traditional fit. That was the style, and we were out in front of it. Those form-fitting Levi's jeans, the muscle tees, the tailored sports coats, the collared shirts . . . that wasn't our market. That wasn't what our clothes were about. We were a little looser, a little more all over the place, a little more casual. And we reflected what was going on in the clubs, in the streets of our communities. It happened in a blink, which is about the time it now takes for every seismic change on the cultural scene; and in the clothing business, we quickly realized, if you wait for that blink you might miss something; what's hot one moment or one season is on the 2-for-$5 rack at the Salvation Army the next.

Very quickly, then, you started to see kids sacking their pants down past the crack of their butt, exposing their boxers underneath, looking a little less pressed and creased but still styling, still caring about their appearance. Or you'd see some kid swimming in a huge shirt that looked like it could fit a couple of his boys at the same time. It was a cultivated look and it reached all the way up the line, to the top rap and hip-hop artists of the moment, and even on up to the NBA—which to a kid from Hollis, Queens was like Hollywood royalty. Look back at video from early in Michael Jordan's career and check out those tighty-whitey type shorts they used to wear, and compare that to the baggy, below-the-knees look they were wearing by the time he retired. It's like the uniforms went in for a complete redesign, and the shift reflected what these top athletes had gotten used to wearing when they were ballin' back in the 'hood.

There are a couple theories on why this style took hold. The first says that the low-pants look had its roots in the inordinately high rate of incarceration in the African American community. It was a jailhouse look, the theory went. You couldn't keep belts or strings in your cell because you might hang yourself, so your pants would ride low and you'd develop this cocky jailhouse shuffle to go along with the look. I never bought into this, because if you'd look at pictures of kids in their prison garb, the stuff was actually pretty form-fitting. Plus, it had always been the case, that you couldn't wear a belt in the joint, so this one strikes me as a kind of urban fashion legend, that this style would just catch on, all of a sudden.

Another theory was that inner city black kids were so poor they were used to wearing clothes that didn't quite fit just yet. A big brother or cousin or some kid across the street would grow out of a shirt or a pair of pants, and it would get handed down before the next kid in line might have been ready for it, but he'd start wearing it any-way. Over time, you started to see kids wear their big brother's clothes with some pride and swagger, even if the item didn't exactly fit, and soon enough a style took off. This one makes a whole lot more sense to me, from a sociological perspective, although here too there was nothing really new—kids had always gotten hand-me-downs from their older siblings and cousins, so this alone couldn't have accounted for the swing.

There's still another line of thinking that our clothes got looser and baggier to accommodate whatever else we were into at the time. I'll give you an example: graffiti-tagging was a giant big deal in New York, throughout the 70s and 80s, just as it was in other urban areas around the country. If you were into it you'd be running around with all these tall cans of spray paint, and you needed a place to put them in your pants or in your jacket without looking like you were packing. So among a certain group of kids who were big into graffiti, loose pants with big, deep pockets were the hot thing, or big bubble coats that could hold all those cans without bulking up the look of an already bulky garment.

And here's another take: you had all these kids break-dancing and rapping and hip-hopping to a distinctly new beat, in such a way that they might bust out of their clothes if they fit too tight. All of a sud-den, you needed a little room to move—out on the dancer floor or down on the blacktop—and it's possible the clothes got a little bigger as a result. Keep in mind, it wasn't just a New York City phenome-non, this move to a looser style of clothing; it wasn't even necessar-ily urban; early on, some of our biggest sales blips were to skateboarders in Seattle, and break-dancers in Japan, so you never could tell what would catch on, or where, or why.

My theory is that it was all these things taken together—the hand-me-downs, the graffiti, the break-dancing, maybe even a piece or two of the prison legend—mix-mastered with the fact that we finally had a little bit of money to demonstrate our own sense of style, and at the other end you had Karl Kani, Walker Wear, Cross Colours and these other early lines, reinforcing this new trend. Anyway, that's the look we inherited, the look we built on, the look we meant to make our own.

>> STOREFRONT AND CENTER

One of the great benefits of our association with Samsung was supposed to be the company's deep pockets to help us extend our reach into traditional forms of advertising, but our first efforts in this area were anything but high-end. In fact, our very first marketing push was a street-level effort that cost so little we could have mounted it ourselves, without any of our backers' money.

Our "campaign," if you could even call it that, wouldn't have worked anywhere but big cities, where storeowners have these ugly reinforced security gates they pull down in front of their doors and windows when they close up for the night. We've all seen these pulled-down gates, they're terrible eyesores, and I hit on the idea of spray-painting our FUBU logo on the gates of about 50-75 mom-and-pop type retail outlets throughout the city.

It was a win-win set-up, the way I saw it. And happily the storeowners must have seen it the same way, because not a single one of them turned me down when I pitched them the idea. We went in and cleaned up these metal gates, which the store owners loved, slapped some colorful artwork on them and called it a billboard.

It cost about $200 to do each gate. You couldn't touch that kind of penetration with any kind of traditional advertising, not for that money. I went out and did most of the gates myself—usually at night, usually with an assistant. The drill was I'd throw on a coat of plain silver to use as a background, then I'd paint out a stencil of our FUBU logo, and add the phrase "authorized dealer." It actually looked pretty sexy—much better than the rusted, graffiti-stained corrugated metal I was painting over.

One by one, we had these little marketing outposts positioned in key neighborhoods all over the city—and eventually down into Philadephia as well. And I'll tell you, it was a powerful tool, because after six or seven o'clock, when these stores closed up for the night, we'd be in full view of every bus, car, taxi and pedestrian who happened to pass. Same thing happened the next day, during the morning rush, because most of these stores didn't open until ten or eleven o'clock, so we hit a whole other demographic. The beauty part was that it didn't cost much beyond time and supplies, and it reminded me that even when you do have some deep pockets to underwrite an advertising campaign sometimes the best way to get the word out is on the cheap, on the fly, on the down low.

I'll spend a little bit of time here on the money we started to make, because that's one of the first things people ask me about, what it's like to go from scraping together enough money to cover the rent and the electric bill to having more money than I could think how to spend. Let me tell you, it's not a bad problem to have, but the truth is the money meant more to me than what it could buy. Don't get me wrong, the money was great, but in the beginning I looked on it as a way to keep score, to measure our success. It was a kind of validation, a signal that our concept for these clothes had taken hold, that our decision to throw in with the Weisfelds had been a good one, that we had every reason to expect a bright future.

And that future was upon us before we knew it. I sold the house on Farmers Boulevard about six months into our distribution deal. We'd moved the factory operation out of there early on, and my boys took turns moving out into places of their own, but I stayed on for a while because it was bought and paid for, and because it was what I knew. After a while, though, the FUBU line got so popular, and I became so closely associated with it in my neighborhood, that people were coming to the house at all hours. It was like a local shrine—the place where FUBU got off the ground. People were looking for free merchandise, or to stick us up, or just to hang.

Pretty quickly, the money got in the way of almost every personal relationship I had. Well, maybe not *in the way*, but it became part of the conversation, part of the dynamic. I started to realize that everybody I knew had a $5,000 problem. It's funny, but that was always the amount. First couple months, when people first got the idea that we were making money, they'd hit me up for $100 or maybe $1,000, but that $5,000 number took hold soon after that. There must have been some meeting, somewhere, and everyone agreed on that figure. Anything more, and I'd probably turn them away. Anything less, and they'd come away thinking they could have squeezed me for more.

"Hey Daymond," they'd usually begin. "Can I talk to you? Was wondering if you could help me out."

Then there'd be a whole song and dance over what the money was for—a legit business deal gone bad, back rent, some missed car payments, sick mother, bail, whatever . . . Craziest story I heard was from someone who'd gotten his girlfriend pregnant and needed it for an abortion, but the sick part was he'd claimed she already had an abortion and the doctors left behind the baby's arm. The guy actually said he needed the money for a second operation, so they could remove the arm before it got rotten and infected.

Needless to say, I let this one slide, but as often as not I kicked in. If it was someone I knew really well and I wanted to help out I'd say, "How much do you need?"

"Five thousand dollars," they'd say. Without fail. That was the number. And they'd hold their hands out like it was meant to be a loan, but of course I'd never see any of that money back. And as FUBU continued to prosper, and I had money to give, I gave it freely, without any strings attached. I never fooled myself into thinking I would see that money again, or that these people would find some way to pay me back in kind.

That first year, after the money started kicking in, I think I gave out maybe $50,000 in loans. Then the money got a little bigger, so I got a little more generous. Each year after that, I gave out about $200,000. Family. Friends. Friends of friends. And nobody ever paid me back. But then I realized I couldn't give out money like this forever. It had to end somewhere, so I started saying no. Didn't matter what the request was, or who was doing the requesting, my default answer became no, and it cost me a lot of friendships. You know, people heard I'd given money to so-and-so, and they couldn't understand why I wouldn't give the same money to them. But it had to end, and do you know what? Those $5,000 problems, people somehow got past them. They survived. Don't know if those money troubles went away or got put on hold or what, but they weren't life or death. People managed.

>> MY BODYGUARD

Yeah, I have a bodyguard. His name is Grim. He's my constant shadow. Has been since 1997, right after we hit big. He tells me to stay away from an event, for whatever reason, I stay away. He knows his business. He'd been on tour with everyone from Def Comedy Jam to The Rolling Stones, was likely considered the best at what he does, thought he was giving up that hectic, itinerant lifestyle when he got down with me. But it's been insane. None of us expected it.

There's a downside, though. I walk into a room with a bunch of executives, Grim's got my back, these guys look at me like I'm some kind of thug. Who knows, maybe they'd look at me that way with or without a bodyguard, but that's the first impression I make, The thing is, soon as word got out that we were making money, I didn't feel safe. It was reported one year that we made $350 million, and people must have thought I had all of it under my bed, with the number of times my house was broken into. There were extortionists coming 'round. My family was threatened. Plus, at any given time, I could be walking around with $200,000 worth of jewelry. So why not have a bodyguard? It isn't a power thing, or a gangsta thing. It isn't a show of strength. It's peace of mind.

My boy Grim is an ex-Navy Seal and a martial arts Grand Master. He's disciplined. Doesn't drink. Doesn't smoke. Doesn't party. And he knows that when I drink or party he may have to stop me from getting into a conflict because he knows it could cost me millions of dollars to settle a resulting lawsuit. A lot of celebrities hire friends who are in it just to party. That's why a lot of rappers get shot, or get into unnecessary trouble. Hire the best, that's my position. And Grim is absolutely the best. Bar none.

So there were all these well-meaning people coming out of the woodwork, seeking me out at the house on Farmers Boulevard, coming to me with their hands out, and then on top of that there were all these no-accounts, merely looking to pinch something for themselves, without even the pretense of asking for a loan. It got to where I couldn't live there anymore, much as I might have wanted to, so I sold the house and moved to a condo in Bayside, probably less than 10 miles away. I was still in Queens, still hanging on the same streets I used to roam as a kid, still running with the same crowd, but I was living in a nice place and surrounding myself with nice things and generally enjoying some of the finer things that came with life on a halfway decent starting salary.

There was an old Jewish guy named Hal, part of Norman's sales force, kept his eye on us soon as we started coming to the office. He could see we were onto something. He could see the potential. And every time I'd see him in the hallways he'd say, "Kid, save your money." That's it. Just, "Kid, save your money." I wish like hell I'd listened to him, and I thank God we still have a strong business, because it's extremely easy to spend it all. The lifestyle we lead, the contrast to how we all grew up . . . if we weren't careful, the money could have changed nearly everything.

A funny sidebar on Hal, long as I'm on it. In the garment industry, people use the expression "on wheels" to describe a deal that could come back to you—meaning, essentially, that the other party could give back whatever it was at any time. So Hal had the habit, whenever you asked him to walk you through a sale, he'd say it was on wheels with his pants rolled down, which is how it sometimes goes in every business, right?

We didn't go crazy with the money just yet. That would come. From the get-go, J got himself a little Jeep, so we could load it up with samples and run around to all these video sets. I got a hot new Lexus. (This was around the time I got stuck for my car in Rockville Centre, out on Long Island, visiting my girlfriend.) Wasn't just me, with a fine new ride. We all grabbed something to drive, and we started working ridiculous hours. We lived to work, just about, to get this line up and thriving. I would sleep in the office half the time. Years later, I would take a place just across the street, so I could crash when I was working late, but back then I'd just find a comfortable place to stretch out for a couple hours, grab some sleep and get back to it.

>> OVER-BALLING

We had our own name for early spending sprees. Over-balling. Don't know who came up with that one, but we all knew what it meant because we all suffered from it. Those first checks would come in, and there'd be more zeroes at the end of 'em than we'd seen since our high school progress reports, and we couldn't contain ourselves. We used to call it Christmas, every time there'd be a distribution check—and happily for us Christmas came 'round a couple times each year.

My biggest weakness back then was for real estate. I couldn't help myself, I just kept buying houses. On Long Island. In Florida. Upstate New York. Wherever I saw something I liked, in a place I didn't mind being. One of my first trips down to Florida, I ended up buying a baby mansion, and a condominium just a couple blocks away. That, to me, was an investment. I didn't always manage these investments all that well. I wasn't smart enough to rent some place out if I knew I wasn't going to be staying there enough nights each year to justify the carrying costs, but for the most part I made money on these deals. At the very least, I came out whole.

Cars weren't exactly sound investments, though. This was over-balling in the extreme. When me and my partners turned 30, we bought each other new rides. Anyway, that was the idea. J actually bought me a boat, because I already had enough cars. I bought him a Bentley. Carl got a Corvette, and Keith got a S500 Mercedes Benz. We never thought we'd make it to 30, so it was something to celebrate, but there was always something to celebrate. Cars, jewelry, Cristal, over-the-top parties and press junkets . . . we spent a ton of money we could never get back, but we were having too much fun to regret it. It was all so new, so fresh, so ridiculous, it's like it wasn't real.

Best example of the ridiculous excess that kicked in before we got used to having money: I went out to the store one day and asked my guys if they wanted me to pick anything up for them. They of course said yes (they always said yes), except on this trip the store turned out to be a Mercedes Benz dealership—so I ended up buying that S500 for Keith, just so I wouldn't come home empty-handed. Like I said, ridiculous. Crazy ridiculous, but the money ran straight from our pockets to our heads.

There was a six, seven month period in there after we signed the distribution deal when we were all in a weird kind of holding pattern, almost like a transition. The money started rolling in, and we couldn't spend it fast enough, but we kept our focus at work. We kept at it. We basically went from being this raggedy crew of designers to a legitimate, high-end outfit, all in the time it took to sign our deal, and naturally there were some growing pains. There were also a lot of firsts—like our first distribution checks, our first trips to Europe and Asia, our first significant hires outside our core group, and on and on.

Let me explain about those distribution checks, because I don't want it to come across like Bruce and Norman were doling them out as they felt like it. That wasn't how things were set up. Here's how it worked: as I wrote earlier, me and my FUBU partners retained full ownership and control of the FUBU brand. We were our own separate entity. And then, alongside us, there was Norman and Bruce and their associates, Alliance Worldwide, which in the beginning was under-written by their Samsung corporate parent. Then, we created a kind of holding company for the two companies called GTFM—which stood for,

Get the F***ing Money!—which we split down the middle. We had a whole formula worked out, for how much money we'd set aside against orders, and inventory, and for operating expenses and future capital expenses, and whenever that number was met we'd take whatever was left and call it a bonus. And each time out, that's truly what it felt like—a bonus.

It was a nice set-up on both sides of the deal, and I give all credit to Norman and Bruce for having the courage to consider it. Actually, it was their idea. I was prepared to do the first deal they offered us, the standard distribution deal, but when our signals got crossed the scales tilted a little bit in our favor. When you think about it, it's a remarkable thing, the way they threw in with us. They had a family business. They had about six people in the office, including their sister, Pam, and a couple salesmen. They did bubble coats, and that's it. Then they struck some kind of deal with Samsung, to head up this giant company's apparel division, but they kept their little family business on the side. And that's just what it was when we hooked up, a little family business, and still they opened their doors to four young black guys, who in turn hired another ten black guys, and right away the culture of the place was transformed. It was still a family business, but all of a sudden it was a blended family. We went to all their weddings and Bar Mitzvahs. They came to all our celebrations. They fit us right in.

I don't think I could have done that, if the tables had been turned. Us FUBU guys, we were all so rough around the edges, making it up as we went along, but we had some rope. We were in charge of our own budget. We ran our own show. The Weisfelds put a lot of faith in us, and I was determined to pay it off, but I've got to admit, if I had this nice family business, I would never have allowed these four strangers off the street, let along four black guys I didn't know to come into my life, to put my money and balls on the table and say to them, "We're gonna roll with you."

You don't see this kind of partnership too often, and when you do it's worth noting. Two different cultures come together, and when each side respects the other as individuals and as types, good things can happen. You see it every now and then in the urban market, like with Russell Simmons and Lyor Cohen over at Def Jam, and when it works it can be extremely rewarding. And yet you don't see it enough. A lot of times, African-Americans will look on at white corporate America and grumble that they don't get a fair shake. And I always think, Well, why would anybody stick their necks out for them? What's the benefit? There's always a certain comfort level when you surround yourself with your own, with what you already know. We're not owed anything by these other cultures, just as they're not owed anything by us, but if we can combine and respect each other and work together we can make one color, green. With FUBU and Alliance Worldwide and GTFM, that's been the formula. Black and white equals green.

It took a while for everyone to get used to each other, to try on how we liked to work, how we might work together. Me and my boys, we got in the habit of coming in to the office around noon or so, and we got some funny looks the first couple weeks, but the truth was we were out into the early morning in the clubs, trying to connect with artists and directors and actors and all kinds of tastemakers that could help our line—and that was only after we'd put in a late night at the office, at the design tables or wherever. We worked hard, we just didn't punch the same clock as everyone else, and it took an uneasy couple weeks to sort through all of that.

Meanwhile, to our own little corner of the outside world, it was business as usual for the time being. The people in the clubs, they still looked on us as the boys from Hollis who were making a name for themselves. The rap and hip-hop artists, they still looked on FUBU as a happening brand. I don't think people outside our own circle had any idea how big we'd gotten in such a short space of time, and this was important because it meant we hadn't lost our cache. We were still on that cutting edge, still on the rise, still just four brothers from the 'hood looking to dress a bunch of other people in loose-fitting, styling clothes they couldn't find anywhere else. And the four of us, we took great pride in showing that African-Americans can export or produce something other than rappers and athletes. Very quickly, clothing designers like FUBU became the number one product of African-Americans. We were voted the second-largest minority-owned company in New York, by *Crain's New York Business*. We could step back and look at what we were doing and appreciate that we were selling hard goods that didn't happen to be CDs or DVDs. As our boy LL used to say, we weren't just dancing for chicken any-more. We were businessmen. We went from picking cotton to sell-ing it, and I hope we made our forefathers proud.

Those first trips were . . . well, a trip. All of a sudden, I was in the fashion business, so I was jetting off to Amsterdam, London, Paris and Hong Kong, and this time I didn't have to use those stand-by American Airlines passes. This time we didn't have to sleep head to toe in the same bed. There's a line we used to kick around in the 'hood, "You're in the NBA now." It meant you hit the big-time, play-ing with the big boys, and it was a line I kept hearing, back of my head. In our case, we went from zero to sixty in just about no time flat. There was no period of apprenticeship, no learning at the heels of an experienced executive. We were making it up as we went along. I remember placing my very first order with my production guy in New York, Mr. Cho, and he said to me, "I don't even know why we're placing this order because maybe you'll sell eight hundred pairs. It's just not worth it." That really pissed me off, but I was a straight up businessman now so I kept my cool. I didn't go off on this guy. I couldn't. We were part of this new blended family. We were in this thing together, so I let his comment kind of hang there, and I look at our sales reports now with a special pride every time our jeans sales spike up a bit. To date, we've moved maybe 30 million pairs of jeans, and Mr. Cho must be eating his words every day, but we joke about it now. And he's still the best at what he does.

>> WHY THE YANKEES ALWAYS WIN

There's a great scene in that Steven Spielberg movie, "Catch Me If You Can," where Christopher Walken tries to explain to Leonardo DiCaprio why the Yankees always win. He basically says, "The other guys cannot stop looking at their stripes."

I've thought about that line a lot. You can take it to mean whatever you want it to mean. To me, it means a couple things. For one, it means that the Yankees are stylin', and if you feel good about your appearance there'll be a certain strut, a certain confidence, a certain self-respect in how you go about your business that it carries over into your performance on the field. Those pinstripes, they're never out of fashion. They're classic. And when you move about with classic threads there's an extra bounce to what you do.

It also means that the Yankees have succeeded in making themselves a brand, and in using that brand to advantage. They wear their success, their history, on their sleeves, and they wear it with such pride and honor it can't help but intimidate. Their competitors take one look at that Yankee uniform, with those Yankee pinstripes, and it starts to play with their heads. They're down in the count before the first pitch is even thrown.

There's a parallel to each of these interpretations in the African-American community, where style also counts, where first-impressions count, where feeling good about yourself and your appearance counts most of all. The clothes you wear, the jewelry you custom-design, the car you drive . . . these things say a lot about you. They announce who you are, where you've been, how you want to be seen. Like when I walk into a room with a gold FB chain around my neck. In some rooms, it's considered gaudy and tasteless; in others, it's an emblem of honor, respect and accomplishment. Some people might not recognize my face, but the FB emblem will never be mistaken. It's my stripes. Yeah, it's a huge shout-out to the money you have in your pocket, but it goes beyond that, I think. We're not just saying, "Hey, I'm rich, so take me seriously." We're saying, "Take me seriously because I care about my appearance, because I take myself seriously." We're saying, "Hey, I stand on the shoulders of a lot of people."

That's the Yankees, man. They take themselves seriously, and they stand on the shoulders of the people who used to wear the same uniform. That's why the other guys can't keep from looking at their stripes—because they represent.

One of the biggest adjustments came in personnel, because obviously the four of us couldn't run this operation on our own. We wanted to do it up right. There was a certain pressure to hire African-Americans, as jobs opened up, although it wasn't really unspoken . . . I heard about it whenever I went another way. See, my thing was to hire the best people for the job. Plain and simple. If it worked out that I could give a brother or sister a boost, that was great. If it didn't, that was great too, because it meant I'd found someone better suited to the job. I'd get all these calls, saying, "Come on, man, hook me up," but if I only hired these come-on-man-hook-me-ups, my business would die and I would no longer be able to help anybody.

It took a while for me to figure out this hiring and firing business, and to set the right tone around the office—one that would allow us to get the most out of our employees and at the same time to stay true to the impulse behind FUBU. We weren't looking for a desk job for ourselves, so we couldn't expect the people we hired to take a drudgery approach to their work. We didn't want 9-to-5ers, phoning it in. We wanted to establish a creative, exciting, hard-charging environment that was also exhilarating and fun—like a party with a purpose. We weren't out to bust anybody's butts, but we were hoping to find good people who would take it on themselves to bust their own.

I came to realize that it takes an employee about two weeks to mimic the way he or she is being treated in the workplace. Treat your staff like crap, and they'll eventually pass it on to your customer. Treat them like gold, and they'll go to the wall for you and your product. Two weeks. That's the honeymoon period. That's the stretch of time you'll usually get in grace, when people are out to please their bosses, no matter how they're being treated. After that, what you put in starts to get put back out. That explains why people behind the counter at the post office or the Department of Motor Vehicles can be so sour and unhelpful. They hate their jobs. Same with some cops, and other civil servants. You see it in the retail sector as well, with minimum-wage type hires putting minimum-wage type effort into their service, which is why we tried to pay our top people as much as we could afford instead of as little as we could get away with, to keep our staff as happy and productive as possible.

>> GO DIRECTLY TO JAIL

One of the routines I developed, early on, was to sit my people down for a game of cut-throat Monopoly—once a month or so, after hours. For a while, we played a couple times a week. It was a great release from all the tension and pressure that would build up during the day, and more than that it turned out to be a chance to see the people who worked for you outside of a traditional office dynamic.

Think about it: around a Monopoly board, you can see how sharp someone is, how they deal with people, whether they're hesitant or honorable. It's a great tell. Didn't start out like any kind of strategy or litmus test. A group of us just started playing, is all, and I started to notice the value in the game, started inviting others to sit in, on a rotating basis.

Understand, it wasn't a garden-variety game of Monopoly, the kind you used to play when you were a kid. No way. This was vicious. We'd play for money sometimes—maybe $50, maybe $100, whatever we felt like at the time—but it was never about the money. This was killer, full-throttle Monopoly, and it was all about winning. It was about pride and respect and bragging rights, and whatever it took to outplay, out-smart, out-hustle your opponents.

Over time, the game cost a couple people their jobs, or maybe even made a couple careers. Don't mean to suggest that I made my hiring and firing decisions based on a board game—but hey, I'd learn some things that colored my thinking. I mean, you play ten games with someone, and they're constantly cheating or being slick, you start to question whether they're the type of person you want representing you or your company. Conversely, you play ten games with someone, and they're making deals and working it out and finding a way to win, you take notice of that too, and maybe you fast-track someone as a result. You lean towards what you see around that board. You play with a guy, he doesn't know how to pull the trigger, he can't see all the way down the road, takes a very short view on things, you make a note. You see a guy, can't take the pressure, gets mad when things don't go his way, starts to throw things, you make a note of that as well.

Yeah, it's just a game, but a lot of people think business is just a game, too. We're all playing to win. With Monopoly, it's the kind of game that reveals a person's character. Chances are, it's stuff that would come out eventually, but it puts a clock on eventually and gives you information you'll need to get and keep ahead. And it doesn't have to be Monopoly. It could be anything. Poker. Hoops. Pin The Tail on the Donkey. This is why rich white guys spend so much time on the golf course, doing deals. Find whatever works for you and your group and make something out of it. And be sure to take notes.

I looked up one day and counted over 200 people working for us, in one capacity or another. At one point, with all our licensees, it got to over 300, and I realized that it takes being an employer of a fairly big operation to recognize that there are a lot of people out there who major in minor things. I can't take credit for that line—it's Tony Robbins's—but soon as I heard it I thought, That's the truth. People go about their business in their individual ways, and a lot of them spend a little too much time on the small stuff and not nearly enough time on the big picture, and it fell to me and my boys to figure out which personalities to match with all the different things that needed to get done as we grew our line. Even among the four of us, we all had our strengths and weaknesses, the things we liked to focus on, the things we would just as soon let slide, but our performances weren't necessarily up for review. We answered to each other, and we balanced each other out.

It was in filling out our ranks that we sometimes got into trouble—because let's face it, we didn't always get it right. Sometimes it fell to me to let one of our people go. I can still remember the time I lost my firing virginity—the first time I had to fire someone. I didn't really have a frame of reference for this kind of thing. I'd been fired once, from my part-time job at the popcorn stand back when I was a kid, and in that case the guy simply discovered that the register was short by a couple dollars so he said, "Get the hell out of here, you're fired." Can't imagine he obsessed about it. He just fired me. But when it came time for me to pull my first trigger, I was all bent out of shape about it. I'd hired this guy as a designer, and he was talented enough, but after he'd been with us a while I could see he wasn't what we needed. He had a good attitude, and a positive energy, but he just couldn't execute the way I would have liked. I gave him every chance to turn things around, figured maybe it would just take him a little time to get caught up in our style, but there came a time when I had to admit it wasn't working out. So I called him in, and of course he was smiling, and up, and positive, and I said, "I've got to let you go."

Took this guy completely by surprise. His face just turned. He got short of breath. He had a family. Two kids, wife, house, mortgage . . . the whole deal. He panicked. He was worried how he'd make ends meet, and I tried to set him at ease, send him off with a reasonable package, promise to hook him up someplace else. And I think if he was honest he would have agreed that this hadn't been a good fit, but it was still hard. And this was firing a good person, someone who meant well. The screw-ups, they were always an easy fire. If anything, I'd be a little too quick to let these idiots go. Someone would set me off, or I'd get it in my head that they weren't as focused as I was, I'd want to fire them immediately. Keith would have to stop me. He had a little more experience in corporate leadership. He'd tell me to calm down and take a longer view.

>> I FIRED OPRAH

Sometimes, it's the road not taken that gets you where you're meant to go. Despite our early successes, and despite the fact that we'd been written up in virtually every major publication and interviewed on every major news program, we couldn't get a break from Oprah. We thought that would just put us over the top, you know, an appearance on the Oprah Winfrey show, and it was a real puzzle to me, why she wouldn't put us on.

In many ways, this was the first marketing or promotional nut I couldn't crack, and I couldn't think what to do about it, and around 1999 we hired a young woman in public relations who happened to be Oprah's relative. It wasn't a strategy, hiring this woman; we had no idea she was related to Oprah. And when I did find out, I never came out and asked her to work those family ties on FUBU's behalf; I tried to respect her privacy.

Even so, she was plugged in to Oprah's star power, because this woman would be at red carpet events before me and my boys. She'd be at premieres and major concerts, sitting in the front row, while I was back in the fourth or fifth. She was everywhere. Only trouble was, she wasn't really on top of her job, so the dilemma became, What do I do about Oprah's relative? We were already having a tough time getting a hearing from Oprah's producers. We had a shot to be on the show early on, but they wanted to bring cameras by the house, and shoot video of me and my family, and all the bling that supposedly came with our success, and I didn't want to open up those doors in such a public way. So that first opportunity fell away, and we couldn't get on as businessmen or intellectuals talking about the hip-hop marketplace, and I had to think that firing the woman's relative wouldn't exactly help our chances. But the fact remained, she wasn't the right person for the job. Nothing against her, but we needed to make a change.

I thought about it, and I thought about it, and I realized that if Oprah knew the situation, she probably wouldn't want her relative getting some kind of free pass, just because of her famous family connections. (That's why she probably didn't work for Oprah.) So it became clear we had to fire this person, and as I did so I couldn't shake thinking there'd be some kind of fallout. But the thing is, the fallout was all to the good, because we ended up making a lot of noise on Montel Williams's show, and that was just fine with us. So we went ahead and booked Montel's show, and he and I hit it off. Now we hang, we go snowboarding at his place in Utah, and he's become a huge inspiration to me. We've since been on his show a bunch more times, and we've done some great things—like give away a million dollars worth of clothes on his program to people in and around New Orleans, just after the devastation of Hurricane Katrina.

So there we were, with no more inside track to Oprah, a good friend now to one of her competitors, and I allowed myself to build up all this resentment towards this woman—the same resentment that ran through a lot of the hip-hop community, because it was felt she was boycotting rappers on her show. Now of course I realize full well that she probably never even knew we were trying to get on her show, but this is how I built it up in my head. I'd hear people talking, how Oprah is prejudiced, how she doesn't like rappers, and this and that, and I'd buy into it. I'd fuel those same rumors—because, after all, she'd never given us the time of day. And then she comes out and does this "Legends" special, paying homage to twenty-five influential black women like Diahann Carrol and Lena Horne and Coretta Scott King, women who had inspired her for whatever reason. She also highlighted another twenty-five "young 'uns"—women like Tyra Banks and Naomi Campbell, and she put herself in that category, saying she's no spring chicken but still young in comparison to these other legends. That one show opened the eyes of a new generation to some of the most ground-breaking women of our time. It couldn't have been done any better.

I looked on at home and couldn't help but be inspired. Just from that one show, I started to see that there were a lot of similarities between me and Oprah, in the way we ran our lives and our companies. I'd allowed myself to build up all this anger towards her, and chances were she had no idea there was anything going on between us. It reminded me of all the grief we used to get over at FUBU, about not being black-owned, about not giving back to our community. You know, it's easy to throw pebbles at an elephant, and I wasn't giving her the respect she deserved.

I still haven't been on her show, by the way, but now I don't blame Oprah for it—and I don't blame the fact that I had to fire her relative.

Hiring was also tricky. My thing was to let people surprise you. You know, give someone a chance. If I had a gut feeling about someone, I'd usually offer them a spot, even if there was nothing in their background to suggest they were the best qualified for the job. Early on, I brought in some of my boys from Red Lobster, and that didn't always work out, but I liked to bring in people who were hungry, people who appreciated the opportunity, because I put myself on their side of the desk and realized I'd work double-time to reward the benefit of the doubt. If someone put that kind of faith in me, I'd be sure not to disappoint.

You never know where you'll find your next asset. My president of marketing, Leslie Short, has been a Godsend, and she wasn't anywhere near the FUBU picture when we first started out. In fact, she used to work for my boy Montel, as one of his producers, and before that she was a ballet dancer in Europe and Asia, but now I can't imagine running our business without her insight and inspiration. It's like she came out of nowhere, and we'd be nowhere without her.

My head designer right now is a woman named Simone Newbolt, and she started as an intern, not long after we were up and running. Now I can't live without her. She's like my right arm. There's also Malcolm Wilson, my personal assistant, who keeps me organized and moving forward. Before Malcolm, there was Anthony Ballard— Tony, my old bike shop partner from when we were kids—and he was more than my assistant. He was my driver, my housekeeper, my babysitter, my accountant. And Joe Levin, my head salesman, who really gets the FUBU message and helps us to put it out there.

A lot of our best people started as interns. They'd work for six months, maybe a year or two, and the expectation was they would dedicate themselves to their jobs as if they were being paid, and if they performed well they'd graduate to some kind of paying position. That was the unspoken bargain. But at FUBU, we had a pretty rigid salary structure. We'd start our people out at, say, $30,000, and sooner or later, given the popularity of our brand, some other designer would try to hire someone away from us and offer, say, $50,000. We couldn't match that. We tried to, in the beginning, and people went from $30,000 to $100,000, and when you spread that kind of money around among a couple dozen of your senior people, your payroll gets a little crazy. One year it was $3 million, the next year it was $7 million, the next year it was $9 million. It didn't make any sense.

This kind of thing got a little ugly—not because our good people would leave, which I guess was inevitable, but because they'd get mad that we couldn't match their outside offer, which I guess was unavoidable. My thinking was, Hey, if you can do better someplace else, then go someplace else. But underneath that thinking was a certain disappointment. I mean, we took these people on, gave them an opportunity, trained them, and then someone comes along and makes them a better offer and they're out the door. They'd say, "Daymond, I worked that first year for free, and after that I was only making thirty thousand!" And I couldn't really counter that, except I might have pointed out that I could have hired a person with experience, who would have come to FUBU with a bulging Rolodex, who would have brought us more business, but people don't hear that when you lay it out for them. They don't hear that we were making an investment in them, that you gave them an opportunity. They hear what they want to hear, and what they wanted to hear from me is that I would match their outside offer. (But of course, that outside offer wouldn't exist if they didn't have the FUBU name, training and contacts behind them.)

My issue wasn't over the fact that they'd leave, but that they'd go out the door saying the FUBU guys were the worst employers on the planet. What was *that* about? If it was me, I'd have played it differently. First off, I might have been a bit more loyal, and hung in with the company that gave me my first shot. But even if I did reach for that bigger paycheck, I'd have gone in to the person who hired me and said, "Thanks. I learned a lot from you. I wouldn't be where I am today were it not for you." That's the class move, right? Instead we usually got a little bad-mouthing as these people made their way out the door, and we had no choice but to take it because it would have cost us dearly if we broke from our salary structure. Why? Because employees speak to each other. They compare notes—and paychecks. There's bitterness and jealousy if someone at the same general level as someone else is making a bigger salary. Our thing was, we'd pay you to come back. If you left FUBU and we tried to hire you back, we might have to set our salary structure aside, but we couldn't go matching every offer that came in from a headhunter looking to lure away our good people.

We couldn't chase everyone. Some of the ones who got away went on to bigger and better—or, at least, on to something different. If you look at the people who have been out in front of the rise to prominence of the hip-hop movement—people like Spike Lee (40 Acres and a Mule), Hype Williams, Andre Harrell (Uptown Records), Russell Simmons (Def Jam), Jermaine Dupri (So So Def), J. Prince (Rap A Lot), Dr. Dre, Puffy (Bad Boy) and me and my FUBU boys, along with the editors of *Source* and *Essence* magazine, we've probably employed thousands of talented African-Americans over the years. Chances are, if you're young and black and making some noise in the entertainment and fashion industries, you came through one of our doors—and I'm proud to have played my own small part in the development of so many influential careers in the urban market, even if some of these people have gone on to make their marks someplace else.

>> WINDOWS ON THE WORLD

There got to be such a mixed-bag of people working for us at FUBU that we began to look like the United Nations. We didn't plan it that way, but that's how it shook out and over time it got to be like a sitcom in our board room. We had the black guys who worked in design, promotion and sales;

the Koreans who worked with the vendors; the Indians in manufacturing and production; the Jews who worked in sales and finance; and on and on.

We all got along, but the culture clash could be hilarious, and it took a while for us to learn each other's angles. For me and my boys, a lot of the difficulties came over food. At least, that's what we were told. Sounds stupid, I guess, but it got to be a big deal. We'd be sitting around a conference table, working through lunch, and we'd sit down around our plate of food like someone was looking to steal it from us. And if someone did grab a forkful without our permission, we'd go off on them like they'd hit on our sister. In our 'hood, you just don't go digging in people's things, but in some other cultures it's obviously cool, among friends, to just go digging in without even asking.

We took our food seriously, probably because there wasn't always enough of it to go around when we were kids. And you had to watch us on this, because we'd grab your food like we had it coming. It was a one-way street, far as we were concerned. Some of our Jewish guys were fairly religious, and they'd have prayers up in the office on some days, and we figured out pretty quick that they had food laid out for afterwards, so you'd have all the black guys waiting outside the conference room so we could swoop down on those platters as soon as their prayers were over, so we could kick in the door and get our grub on.

The Koreans, they had their own way of doing business. I'd tell my main production guy Mr. Cho that I wanted a garment done up in purple, this length, and delivered on a certain date, and because he would have to interpret to some of the factories in Korean he would take liberties and for all I know say Daymond wanted it in black, longer, and delivered on whatever date he felt worked best. I'd talk to him in English, and he'd spread the word in Korean, and I'd have to take it on faith that he was following my orders. Sometimes he was, sometimes he wasn't. And when he wasn't, I learned, he wasn't being disrespectful. He just had his own ideas on seniority. Who do you listen to, if you're a 55-year-old Korean male? Probably not a 35-year-old black guy, right? So we had to move a little bit sideways with these guys, because they don't necessarily listen to the people who sign the checks. It's about seniority.

And there's a whole gender thing going on there as well among Korean women, where the senior female is known as the "Annie," an honorific based on age, not on value to the company, so we had to learn that when we were dealing with the Koreans we couldn't have a younger, higher-ranking female employee give any kind of directive to an older underling, because it just wouldn't fly. And an older male is totally out of the question.

It's just a different corporate culture, a different mindset. Like the Indians who work with us.

The outside of my house on Farmers Boulevard that would be my first factory.

The living room . . . for cutting material.

The bedroom . . . for packing goods.

The dining room . . . where one of my machine operators was sewing garments.

ARE YOU READY TO BE AN ENTREPRENEUR?

One of our first hangtags. Stores would not carry our product.
They thought we looked like a gang.

We didn't look very menacing to me!

These are one of the normal parties where we would give the crowd an estimated 50 bottles of Cristal at $1,000 a bottle to show our appreciation to our customers. At one point we were throwing ten or more of those parties each year. (Perhaps the Cristal owners should have done the math on those!)

The Indy 500. In the race car (above) and at a press conference (below). Unfortunately, our FUBU car crashed in the fifth lap, but we were one of the first black-owned companies in the Indy.

The Greatest.
Me and the "World's Most Recognizable Living Person"
Muhammad Ali!

He came to my office to say thank you and to approve some
of the FUBU product with his likeness on it.

This is a picture of me trading him a FUBU watch for the watch
on his wrist. I now have it framed and it hangs on the wall behind
my desk. It is one of my most valuable possessions.

This is how
we do it
internationally.

Here I am with everyone's silent partner (Russell Simmons).
He was the first rich guy I saw driving around Hollis, Queens
who wasn't selling drugs.

To my right is "The Donald." I knew
the day I was escorted out of his offices while on a delivery
that one day I would meet him on my terms.

They'd shake their heads "no" when they meant "yes," but we all figured each other out eventually. We all learned not to take ourselves too seriously—because, in the end, we were all after the same thing.

A lot of managers and executives are held hostage by their employees because they don't know their own business. They've never worked the line. At FUBU, we knew the drill from the ground up, because we'd done it all. Me and my boys, we worked the mail room. We cut fabric. We designed new lines. We came up with the marketing plan. Even as the big money started to roll in, we did it all—and we still do it all. We're constantly out there, working alongside our people, putting in the same effort we expect from each of them, and I happen to think it's a powerful motivating tool. That's not why we do it, necessarily, but it is a great side benefit. It puts it out there that we don't place ourselves above the work, that the success of our line is paramount, that we'll do whatever it takes to succeed. Also, we don't take our success for granted. We don't ask our people to do anything we wouldn't do ourselves, anything we haven't already done a hundred times over.

That's something I learned back at Red Lobster. The thinking there, at the corporate level, was that managers needed to know every aspect of the operation. That was the only way to know if anyone was stealing from them, the only way to know how everyone was managing their time, the only way to know what areas needed to be improved. Plus, it's the only way to CYA. If a cook or anybody on the line suddenly quit at six o'clock on a Saturday night, just before your big rush, the manager needed to be able to flip back his tie, put on an apron and cover. General Mills owned the Red

Lobster chain at the time, and that was the General Mills approach. They never wanted to be caught short.

I tried to build on that at FUBU—only not by design so much as by necessity. Before we hooked up with Norman and Bruce, we needed to do it all. It was just the four of us, and whatever friends or family members we could rope in from time to time. We needed to design our line, produce samples, sell them at trade shows, fill orders, pack and ship and service our accounts. (Remember, I did most of the sewing myself, on those first couple runs.) By now, we've moved on from me, Keith, J and Carl having to pitch in, but we're still pitching in. We're still on the line. I'm constantly flipping back my tie and getting to work. (No, I don't actually wear a tie, but that's not the point.) Nowadays, though, it's out of habit, and with that habit comes a message, either to my own people or to the people we're doing business with. It sets a positive example. And no detail is too small. For example, I personally go down to the video sets and talk to some of these artists who are wearing our clothes, and whenever I do there's a great windfall. I could just as easily send one of my staff down, but it means a lot when the CEO comes down himself. It means you're taking an interest, down to every last detail. People notice that, and they appreciate it. They say, "You came down here yourself?" And I say, "Yeah, I did. Because you're important to me and to the success of this company."

It's the same with our manufacturers. Maybe they think we beat them up on price or whatever, but when we're out on the road, making the circuit, we make sure we got to the factories, not only to make sure the product is right but to show that we're serious about doing business with them. Dubai, India, Hong Kong . . . Doesn't matter if it's out of our way or deep into the middle of nowhere, I make a point of building and nurturing these relationships, because in the end they're the only thing I've got. They're the only thing covering me in the event that my fry-cook up and quits on me, six o'clock on a Saturday night. This right here is the biggest piece of advice I can give to a young entrepreneur, to learn your business from the ground up. Doesn't matter how low that ground is, but get down and dirty and learn that business before you go anywhere.

>> THE HEAT CYCLE

Here's how it goes sometimes, when you're measuring the life of a popular brand. First couple months, you're at the ground level, and everybody wants in. You might not be making any money, but you're the flavor of the month, the number one record, the talk of the town.

Everybody wants to be in on something new, to be part of a family. Doesn't matter if it's a gang, or a trend, or whatever, there's this groundswell of enthusiasm, and if you get caught up in it there's a sense of belonging. You're part of something special. That's why, even when a record label is introducing a new artist, they'll make sure that artist is popular in his hometown, in some little city, somewhere, because they've learned you can't go national with an act unless it has that hometown base and support. Otherwise, what the hell are you belonging to? With FUBU, we had all these ambassadors in their own 'hoods, guys who bought in to what we were doing in a big way, who took a special pride in being known as "The FUBU Guy" in their small part of the world. That was their thing, and it helped us to do our thing, because they felt a certain pride of ownership, a connection to our brand, and they wanted to pass it on.

The American consumer always wants in, but he wants in to . . . something. And this right here is the crest of the wave, because once that something special is shared with everybody, once it's on the cover of Time or Newsweek or even People, it's not special anymore. In the clothing industry, you can ride that wave from anywhere from two to five years, when you're creating buzz, connecting with the trend-setters and taste-makers and whoever it is that sets the tone. At first, you're just hitting the big markets—New York, Los Angeles, Chicago, Atlanta . . . these days, cities that tend to have a thriving music and modeling industry. After that, it washes over the rest of the country, and you're big with a certain crowd in every market.

Okay, so now you're fiery hot, your inventory has grown, your margins are lower, there are knock-off companies out there looking to undercut your brand, and your core customers have three or four years of your product in their closets. They're ready to move on, but now Middle America has started to pay some attention. Now parents are buying your clothes for their kids. Now you're not as "popular" as you might have been when you were riding the wave, but you're making more money than ever before. The cache is gone, but you're selling way more pieces, only the danger here is that when Mommy and Daddy are buying your clothes, they tend not to be the clothes you want to go out and buy for yourself.

Remember when Von Dutch first hit it big? Ashton Kutcher and a whole bunch of MTV-types started wearing their trucker caps, and Paris Hilton was wearing it all day. They had a flagship outlet on Melrose, and for whatever reason a lot of young Hollywood seemed to tap into it. It was retro. It was low-end done up in high-quality. It had everything going for it. And it was everywhere. At one point, at the tip of the juggernaut, I even thought of buying the company, when we were in a real acquisitions mode. But then they just imploded. They opened a couple stores, and they opened their distribution—and then, almost as quickly as the line had burst on the scene, they slowed down. It's the kiss of death, for a line like that to grow too quickly, to reach into a general market.

So what went wrong? Well, Von Dutch never really changed its core design. They did t-shirts and sweats and hats, with their eyeball-with-wings logo, or the distinctive script "Von Dutch." And because they never changed things up, they made it easy for counterfeiters to come in and pirate their line. They didn't operate enough of their own retail outlets. They lost a little bit of control, which mean they left hundreds of millions of dollars on the table. Plus, their move into these department stores just about sapped the life from the brand, before it had run its course. The better move, the longer-term move, might have been to let those first two phases of the cycle play out, and then start launching different premium brands, as we would try to do as the FUBU brand started to age.

Von Dutch, they got fiery hot and they misjudged the delicate shift you need to make in the market in response to that kind of heat. These days, you either go low, or you go super premium. There's no reason to go to Sears anymore, because you have Wal-Mart and K-Mart and Target, so you can either go down that low road, or aim higher still. And I'm talking really high-end, otherwise you can't differentiate. That's what we did. We launched Platinum FUBU, and following that we bought a premium Australian line called Coogi and repositioned it for our American market. We lifted the quality, and we raised the price, and we set the bar as high as we possibly could, so that we could once again ride that wave. And it wouldn't be quite the same ride you were on initially, but it would be a ride worth taking.

But those Von Dutch guys are smart, and if they hit it big once, they can probably do it again.

That heat cycle was on full blast, almost from the beginning, and I want to shine a light on a couple crazy, hectic, hard-to-believe developments and other related quick hits, just to give just a little taste what things were like in and around the FUBU offices as the line started to take off in a big way.

- We became well-known for our parties and events, like our $4 million, weekend-long Y2K bash in St. Martin, and a two-day concert featuring The Gap Band, Mary J. Blige, Case, Tina Marie and a mess of artists. We gave away a couple hundred bottles of Cristal from the stage (back when Cristal was still politically correct), flew down over a thousand contest winners to take part in the festivities, and generated a ton of good will among artists and celebrities that lasted for the next while . . .

- We'd regularly get letters from families telling us their loved ones had asked to be buried in FUBU clothing. They'd send pictures, to prove the point. Also, on the letters front, we'd hear from white kids who were getting beat up in school for wearing our line, and we'd always send back a poster or some other giveaway with a note reminding the person that FUBU was not about a color, it's about a culture . . .

- The success of FUBU meant the failure of my marriage. I haven't spoken a lot about my wife and children in these pages, because I like to keep that part of my life private, but I think it's important to note that I lost my family during FUBU's climb. Nobody on their death bed says, "I wish I spent more time at the office," but that was me—and it's something you have to understand if you're out to succeed. As much as my wife gave me all the real advice I needed, kept me grounded and focused, we still drifted apart. You can try to keep a healthy balance, as I tried to do, but sometimes the business gets the better of the deal . . .

- In 2001, when a Georgia county school board banned high school students from wearing t-shirts with the symbol of the Confederate flag, a counter bill was proposed banning FUBU garments as well. You had the one symbol of white supremacy, and some functionary decided we were the symbol of black supremacy, like we were a black version of the KKK . . .

- Also in 2001, Senator Hillary Clinton honored the FUBU founders for our dedication to community service in the New York area—marking the first time the former First Lady gave out an award as an elected official . . .

- Similarly, outgoing New York Mayor Rudolph Giuliani presented us with one of the last awards he handed out while still in office . . .

- Remember when I wrote earlier that one of the pipedreams back in the beginning was to get a display in Macy's? Well, we went that one better—getting a Macy's window display on at least a dozen occasions, including a first-of-its-kind, live-action, in-store (in-window!) appearance, with the four of us on display, taking questions from shoppers on the street and posing for pictures . . .

- We made our own splash in the sports world. Throughout Lenox Lewis's heavyweight career, FUBU was on his shorts and in his corner. We outfitted the champ, and put him in our ads, and he became the face of FUBU in the sports arena . . .

- A couple of our founding FUBU guys went to Johannesburg to open our first free-standing store in South Africa, and received a Secret Service-type escort around the city that eventually included a stop to meet Nelson Mandela. South African President, Thabo Mbeki, became so enraged that a separate meet and greet had to be set up with him . . .

- We became the first African-American company to sponsor a car in the Indianapolis 500—another out-of-the-box marketing opportunity. We had a Chilean driver, an Hispanic crew, and our black ownership group, which meant we really stood out in such staid, traditional company . . .

- We were presented with dozens of keys to various cities, and there were several FUBU days around the country, in cities like Detroit and Miami, and I mention them here to show how deeply connected some communities felt to our brand . . .

- And speaking of community, we'd make it a special point, every year at Thanksgiving, to hand out thousands of turkeys all over New York City. It was our way of quietly giving a little something back to the 'hood . . .

- Michael Jackson called up to our offices one day when he was in New York, recording a new album. He was thinking about re-doing his look, so I went down to his studio with a bunch of clothes, and the booth was filled with stuffed animals of every size, color and stripe. And candy! M&Ms and Reese's Pieces. Just shelves and shelves of this stuff. Just for him. We sat around and talked, and Mike seemed to be just a regular guy . . .

- In one of the highlights of my career, FUBU was one of the first companies to receive the *Essence* award, on national television, given by the editors of *Essence* magazine. I can still remember stepping to the podium to receive the honor and thinking, We've finally arrived . . .

- And, my favorite quick-hit, pop culture memory from those heady days of our first successes: when O.J. Simpson came down to the set of the "Fatty Girl" video we were directing with Hype Williams to promote a song on an album we were producing and a spin-off ladies line. Video vixen Karrine Steffans was on the set dancing up a storm, and Ludacris had a chain with handcuffs on them, and O.J. started really getting into it, rubbing up against Karrine, putting the handcuff necklace on, really mugging it up for our cameras. He started talking about how he knew handcuffs really well. (Wow! O.J. in our video with Karrine shaking her booty on him! What a sight!) We never used any of that footage, it was too controversial, but I think back on it as symbolic of the weird, crazy, chaotic life we found ourselves living when things first started popping . . .

We learned the fashion business on the fly. We're still learning. In the beginning, all we knew was what we liked, and how to get our clothes into the hands of the top artists, but we didn't know the first thing about sizing, and seasons, and shipping. Norman and Bruce and them, they had a certain expertise, and they passed what they could on to us, but the rest of it we kind of had to figure out as we moved along. We weren't exactly on our own, but we did have to hit the ground running—and, to be honest, we stumbled from time to time.

Let's start with sizing. One of the first things we had to figure out was how to know how many garments to make in small, medium, large, extra-large. The first few orders we wrote, at that first MAGIC show, the store owners would tell us how many items they wanted in each size, but as we kicked things up a notch we had to anticipate our sizing needs, so we tended to skew large. That was our gut instinct. Eventually, we hit on a formula, but we got there by trial-and-error, and by understanding our market. When was the last time you went down to Disney World? The people you see on line, they're huge, right? We tend to lose sight of that fact, moving about in trendy, fashion-conscious, health-conscious places like New York, Los Angeles and Miami, but most people in this country are over-weight. We're up there. And on top of that we had to figure that among our core demographic, the young African American male, people liked to wear their clothes a little bigger, so we ran our sizes accordingly. Our first couple lines, we ran from XL to 6XL. Of course, our XLs were never a true extra-large, but even here it was all about branding. Our thinking was, No man wants to be reminded that he's short or skinny or whatever. You don't want to be pointing that out by putting "itty-bitty" on their shirts. So we called our smallest sizes XL and everybody was happy.

Me personally, I would never buy a shirt marked "large." I'm not a big guy, but I reach for the double XL, because I like to have a little room to move and because it makes me feel good about myself, and we've learned that other guys are cut the same way. Now, the flip side to this is that white America believes that skinny is better, and that form-fitting is better, so we might have lost a few customers over the years with this type of sizing, but in our community size matters, so that's what we play to.

The factory end of the business was a whole other education, because we needed all kinds of work on our items. There were button factories, and zipper factories. There was a factory where they died the fabric, a factory where they cut the fabric, a factory where they sewed the fabric . . . There could be as many as nine factories involved in the making of a single garment, if you counted embroidery and packing and shipping. It was a lot to track. From time to time, we'd come across a "vertical" factory, which meant they did everything along one assembly line, and that of course saved us a lot of money and hassle, but we couldn't always match our timetable to their schedule so very often we farmed this stuff out to factories all over the world. At any given time, there could be FUBU merchandise being manufactured on every continent on the planet, that's how spread out we were on this.

One of the real eye-openers when we first got into the big-time end of this business was that we would now be sharing assembly-line space with other clothing manufacturers. Abercrombie & Fitch, Tommy Hilfiger, Gucci . . . turned out none of these companies owned their own factories, so we'd have to jockey for space with these guys. The downside to this was that your line was out there for any of your competitors to see, sometimes months before you were ready to take it to the trade, so your designs were sometimes up for grabs. A lot of times, we'd visit one of our factories and notice a competitor's garment we thought might work well with our overall line, and we'd borrow some elements from it and make it our own, and of course we had to assume that the other guys would do the same if they saw something of ours they happened to like.

When you have no control over who eye-balls your product like that, it's tough to guard against counterfeiters and knock-off manufacturers, and that's a whole double-edged sword. On the one hand, you're flattered to have a line that's popular enough to be knocked-off, but it can come back to bite you in a lot of different ways. It can cut into sales of your own product, naturally, but it can also undermine your brand if the knock-off items are of inferior quality. A lot of times, you'll send an item out to a factory with an order of 100,000 pieces, and they'll overrun an extra 100,000 pieces and somehow slip those pieces out the backdoor. Then you have these guys who bring in any and all kinds of t-shirts, and simply stamp them with whatever designer logos are in that season. The majority of this counterfeit stuff never makes it into Macy's or Foot Locker, but you will see it in some of the smaller boutiques, alongside legitimate goods, and as often as not the store owner will have no idea he's carrying knock-offs.

Early on, I took the view that these counterfeit sales didn't necessarily come off FUBU's bottom line, because most of the people who bought these knock-off items on the cheap would never have bought our legitimate, full-price items in the first place. That's how I spun it in my own head. Maybe they weren't shopping in the stores that carried our line, or maybe they couldn't afford our prices, so I tried to put a positive spin on it. I tried to remind myself that each time someone put on the FUBU name—whether it was embroidered onto one of our garments or silk-screened onto a knock-off—they were in one way or another advancing the FUBU brand. They were getting our name out there.

You had to make something positive out of a negative, you know.

Even so, we've tried to bust-up a couple big counterfeit operations over the years, with varying degrees of success. About a year or two after we got our deal, we worked with some New York City police detectives to raid one of the more prominent buildings in the knock-off district on Seventh Avenue, running from 23rd Street to 30th Street, right around the corner from our offices in the Empire State Building. Now, every street vendor in the city knows these buildings. That's where they get their pocketbooks and wallets and books and t-shirts and whatever it is they think they can sell out of a duffel bag, or off a folded-up bridge table. I used to go to the knock-off district myself to buy blanks, first couple times I printed up t-shirts to sell outside the Coliseum Mall. These buildings are open to the public, but there are no signs out front, and the stuff is kind of laid out haphazardly in the offices upstairs, so you have to know what you're looking for.

We'd been trying to get the cops down there for months, and when a couple buddies on the force finally agreed to check it out with us we rented two big U-Haul vans and an 18-wheeler and parked them outside. It wasn't exactly what you'd call a formal investigation. Yeah, the guys we had with us were cops, but me and my boys were also on the scene. We went upstairs and found the FUBU goods and started loading up boxes to take down to the truck. One of the cops said they were confiscating the unauthorized merchandise and produced a piece of paper the owner of the operation was meant to sign. Then a purse belonging to one of the counterfeiters went missing, and things spiraled into ugly right after that. It ended up being a huge mob scene. A lot of people got hurt that day—some of the cops, and even Keith. There were hundreds of people in the streets. The "raid" made the news—but in the end it didn't make much of a dent in the counterfeit operation, and ever since we've learned to grin and bear it, in regard to the knock-offs. It's a fact of life in the garment industry, and if we spent all our time trying to clean out the counterfeiters, we wouldn't have time to design and market our next line, so the trick came in staying one step ahead of these guys, and working only with factories we could trust, where our goods would be protected.

>> DO YOUR HOMEWORK

The surest way to mess up a meeting is to come in unprepared. Guts and instinct are fine, but there's a lot to be said for due diligence and common sense.

Don't find too much of either in the nine-to-five world, I'm afraid. Here's an example: two middle-aged guys came in to make a marketing pitch for our line. They happened to be white. They apparently made a great presentation to Norman Weisfeld, who was interviewing a lot of potential advertising guys for us to consider, and who then arranged for me and our president of marketing Leslie Short to meet with some of his strongest candidates. Everyone was hanging outside our conference room, waiting for the meeting to start, when I bounced in at some point wearing a $100,000 bracelet on one wrist, and a Rolex on my other wrist, and probably a nice gold chain around my neck. Don't know what else I was wearing, but it was probably a pair of jeans. Definitely, not a suit.

I was like a lot of guys from my neighborhood when they first make it big, wearing my money and not buying in to the conventions of the corporate workplace. One of the middle-aged white guys took one look at me, and his jaw dropped. He said, "Wow! What's your position around here?" Then he said, "Whatever it is, they're paying you too much!"

He was just goofing, I imagine, but he missed the mark. His partner put his face in his hands. He knew they were screwed. He knew things had been going well but that they'd just blown their pitch. I wasn't mad or anything, but I couldn't have this idiot doing any work for me. I mean, that's how much of a disconnect he had, to not even know who the CEO was of the company he was pitching, especially at a time when I was on television a couple dozen times each week. To have no idea of the culture of the place, to go off like that razzing a brother about his bling . . . these were not good things.

I flashed Leslie Short a look that meant, This guy has got to go. She knew it was coming. I didn't even have the patience to talk to this idiot, after that kind of start, so I figured she could do it for me. And she did. She said, "Obviously, you have no idea who that just was. That was Daymond John. He's the president and CEO of FUBU, not the white guy you were just talking to. You need to get out of here." Plain and simple and straight to the point—and that point being that you need to figure a couple things out before you put your foot in your mouth.

The other big part of our education, after figuring how to deal with manufacturers and counterfeiters, was learning how to stay ahead of the industry seasons. This one caught me a little bit by surprise, and even today, all these years into it, I still have to look at a calendar to remind myself what season we're working on. I'll walk you through it and you'll get what I mean. Let's say it's March 1st. The biggest date coming up on your calendar is the next MAGIC show, which is coming up in August, where you'll be showing your line that will hit stores the following spring. That's over a full year away, so we really had to start getting out in front and thinking long-term.

During our first couple selling seasons, when FUBU was on the rise, we would have as many as 15 designers working in our New York office—coming up with the designs, the styles, the bodies, the fabrics . . . putting everything on paper. By April, we'd start sending out packages to vendors for bids. These packages would include a computer animated drawing (or, CAD) of what the piece was meant to look like, along with all the materials necessary to make up some samples. All the details go right into that package: how long is the zipper, how long is the crotch, how much we expected to charge for the garment . . . everything.

About a month later, we'd start getting back our first samples. One garment at a time. But remember, we'd given out over a hundred packages, because each season we design far more items than we expect to put into production, so by the middle of June we've made our adjustments and gotten back our second samples from these various manufacturers, and then as we turn the corner into July we put some of our own people to work on some of the finishing touches—sewing the buttons, doing the embroidery, whatever else the design calls for at that point.

Late July or so, we might start to show some of these samples to buyers who come in to our New York showroom, ahead of the MAGIC show, but it's out in Vegas where we expect to do most of our selling. A lot of times, we'll kill a line if it doesn't get a good response at the trade show. A lot of times, a piece might get a lukewarm response at MAGIC but we go ahead with it anyway and it sells through the roof, so you never know. On average, if we take a hundred pieces out to MAGIC, we might kill 20-30 percent of the line, just based on the initial response we'd get from the buyers.

Over time, we've learned that different colors tend to do well for us at different times of the year. This one's kind of obvious, but we weren't always up to speed on obvious. Black sells well no matter what. In Spring, we do a lot of whites, a lot of softer colors like lime and light blue, a lot of traditional colors like navy. In Fall, we might do more oranges, or greens. Common sense stuff, but like I said, we didn't have too much of that going in.

After the August MAGIC show, most of us make a bee-line for Europe, to try to get a jump-start on our next line, and for the first couple seasons this was really the biggest adjustment. With Alliance Worldwide on board, we now had people back in New York who could worry about filling all these new MAGIC orders, while me and my boys could turn our attention to our next line. Used to be, we'd have to skip a season in order to service all our accounts, but all of a sudden we could be fashion-forward. We could try to get a jump on the next big thing before the last big thing even hit stores.

>> THEY WORK HARD FOR YOUR MONEY

A couple years into it, everything was popping. Every few months, it'd be Christmas all over again, and with each distribution check came an extra piece of certainty that we would be at this thing a while. An extra piece of validity for a good, clear concept that we all felt we could build on.

After a while, though, I started to notice that there were certain people out there working harder to knock us down and take our money than we were working to build ourselves up and make our money. Best (or, worst) example of this was a run-in I had with a fairly well known interior decorator.

She'd decorated for a boatload of famous, successful people. Rappers, record executives, Hollywood
types . . . She came highly recommended. But then
I put her to work decorating one of my houses and
to this day almost five years later I have nothing to
show for it beyond litigation papers, after spending
a couple hundred thousand dollars. I didn't even see
a couch or a lamp. And I got to thinking, Okay, so
that's human nature for you. You've got one group
of people working hard to make something out of
nothing, and then you've got another group working
just as hard trying to profit off you, to chip away at
what you've worked so hard to build. There are
people looking to cut you down at every turn, trying
to steal from you, hatching frivolous lawsuits, white-
collar thieves who come up with ways to get you for
more than a million dollars worth of apparel . . . and
we can't touch any of them. You know, it's easier for
me to get a kid arrested for snatching five shirts
from our showroom than it is to prosecute an
employee who fudges numbers, or to go after a factory owner who over-runs our product and sells
the surplus on the side.

Too often, that's the way of it, especially in the
'hood. We want what we want, we reach for what
we can, and we begrudge each other successes we
can't quite make our own. We also look for short-
cuts to our own pots of gold at the ends of our
own rainbows. But there ain't no short-cuts.

SHIFT

The world is changing. The best golfer is black. The tallest basketball player is Chinese. One of the illest rappers is white—and, incredibly, the highest percentage of rap music downloads and CD purchases are made by white females between the ages of 16-25.

Let me tell you, it's harder and harder to recognize the world we actually live in up against the one we still imagine. And the mash-up reaches into every aspect of our popular culture: Lee Iacocca does a series of high-profile Chrysler commercials with Snoop Doggy Dog; Webster's dictionary makes room for street terms like *crunk, hoody* and *Benjamins*; the Academy Award for best song goes to "It's Hard Out Here for a Pimp," by the rap group Three 6 Mafia; and the blockbuster "Matrix" franchise breaks through with a mostly black cast and somehow avoids being labeled and marketed as a "black" movie. For the first time, it's okay for people from all backgrounds to look, dress and aspire to be black. You see it more and more. In Japan, for example, some kids walk about in black face as form of respect or admiration.

Like it or not, there are all kinds of fish in the mainstream these days, but it's not just that the individual players are changing on us. It's not just that we've become more open and accepting and tolerant. It's not just that white kids want to be black, and black kids are grabbing onto traditional "white" brands in bigger numbers than ever before. And it's not just that the exceptions to the rule have taken hold. No, the rules themselves have gone out the window. We're back to making it up as we go along. We've gone from three television networks to three hundred, from a half-dozen outlets for a viable print ad campaign to a couple dozen more besides. We've gone from one national channel for music videos to hundreds of network and local stations that regularly air music programming—not to mention the all-night, all-over play some of these videos get on the club scene. We've gone from traditional wire services like AP and UPI, to niche wire services like Urban Wireless, All Hip-Hop and Sister-to-Sister, up-to-the-minute news organizations that keep our community wired to the latest trends and developments. And we've gone electronic: all of a sudden, the Internet allows for all kinds of back-and-forth, on-demand, real-time interactions with consumers through a direct link into their homes, creating an intimate kind of give and take that would have been unthinkable just a decade ago. This right here has marked the fundamental shift of our generation, for the way it forever changed how "content"—music, videos, movies, television shows, books, even commercials—gets into the hands of consumers.

The stakes have changed as well. Used to be a 30-second spot on BET would cost us about $1,500. This was back in 1998, when most young black kids in America watched BET, but the rates were so low because there weren't any black families with Nielsen boxes in their homes, so the network's numbers hardly registered; really, if you went to any of the projects, in New York, Detroit, Chicago, Los Angeles, you wouldn't find one Nielsen box, which for FUBU meant we could blanket that network for a year for about $1 million. This was huge for us, because BET was like CNN to urban America; it's where we turned for insight and information on everything from politics and business, to clothes and cars and fashion. I mean, we would *own* BET for that $1 million, running our spots ten, fifteen, twenty times a day. We'd usually have about three commercials in rotation, and it was a real bonus for us. It got to where you couldn't sit down to watch that channel without seeing one of our ads. At one point, when I was deep into it and doing a lot of traveling overseas, my wife said she saw me more on television, on BET, than she did at home, and she wasn't exaggerating.

Today, of course, that market is once again out of reach for an upstart company like FUBU. BET has been bought by Viacom, and its 30-second ad rates are now over $6,000, but it's still a steal. Even so, there are so many channels, so many viewing options that everything's diluted. Now you have to be Coke or Apple or Ford to be able to afford the kind of wall-to-wall campaign we put out when we were getting off the ground, but even if you could afford to cough up the money you'd see the penetration is not the same. With TiVO and digital and satellite television, it's easier than ever before for viewers to zap through commercials, so half the time they're not even watching the commercial. And satellite radio networks don't even carry commercials, so that medium is out entirely.

It's hard to know where to spend your ad dollars, if you should even spend them at all. If you're a small company the only way to make the kind of hit we managed is to align with various artists and make your own programming, which is now called branded entertainment. You've got to go at it like we did, only harder. Now you have to place your product in movies, DVDs, television shows, music videos. You have to get product mentions in books, in songs, on television talk shows, in magazine articles. But at the same time you have to be subtle about it. There's a song out as I write this called "Vans," by the rap group The Pack, and the accompanying video was such a blatant plug for the Vans line of skateboarder shoes and clothes you couldn't tell if you were watching a commercial or a music video. In fact, MTV refused to run the video, it was such a shameless tie-in, so there has to be some artistry to it, some flavor. You have to sign on artists, like we did with LL Cool J, and let them carry your flag and build a campaign—wearing your stuff in their videos, talking about it in their songs, showing up on Leno in one of your new shirts, really *owning* your brand in their personal life as well as in their professional life, because that's what young people respond to. They can tell when a star is keeping it real. The consumer knows the drill. They know when you run a commercial the star is getting an endorsement fee, but when he wears it in his private life, the consumer thinks, Hey, this guy can afford to wear anything he wants in the world, and this is what he chooses. That's bigger than any commercial.

Absolutely, you can still break into the marketplace, but the waters of the mainstream have gotten a little more treacherous in the decade or so since we launched our line. You have to hustle, same as always, only more so.

>> BLACK ON BLACK

The annual buying power of African-Americans is more than $680 billion. That's an enormous number, for a market that is typically overlooked. Most of that money goes to housing ($110 billion), food ($53.8 billion), cars and trucks ($28.7 billion), clothing ($22 billion) and health care ($17.9 billion), and that closely parallels the spending in our general population since they cover our basic needs.

In the African-American community, we probably spend a disproportionate amount on electronics and jewelry (and champagne!), but a lot of these are cash transactions and difficult to track, so meaningful figures are unavailable to us on this one. But the really interesting number to me is that we only spend six percent of our money within the black community. Six percent! A lot of people get all hot, when they see a low number like that, but when I break it down I start to think, It's no wonder. It's not like there are any black-owned car companies. Yeah, there are a mess of black-owned dealerships, but that money goes back to Ford or Volkswagon or Toyota, so it doesn't fully count. There might be black doctors, but there are no black hospitals, and last I checked there are no black-owned health insurance companies. Black real estate developers? Probably, but people buy homes based on communities and schools and amenities that have nothing to do with the color of the builder's skin.

My personal take on this is I don't pay too much attention to it. I think about it then set it aside. I'll spend my money within the community if I can, if it makes sense, but basically I'll buy what I need, whenever and wherever I need it, as long as it's reasonably priced. You can't go crazy, trying to keep your money in the black community, because you'll just end up keeping it in your pocket. You go to the car wash, it's run by a white guy. You go to the deli, it's run by a Korean guy. Order a pizza, it's the Italian guy. Your head can explode, second-guessing every purchasing decision.

My professional take, from a marketing perspective, is that there's a need to be filled in many industries, and that there are African-Americans looking to spend their money on African-American products, if only they could find them. There's no such thing as an "urban" line of frozen foods, but maybe there should be. Think about it. Most blacks and Hispanics do their shopping at the local bodega. We don't always have a big Stop 'n Shop in the neighborhood, especially in our inner cities, so our choices are limited. But if Sara Lee or Stouffer's decided to market a B. Smith line of frozen foods, or Fat Joe's meat loaf, or whatever, people would definitely buy it. You know, some kid comes in to the store, he wants something to eat, he likes Fat Joe, he checks out the packaging, he'll definitely buy it. And the people who don't even care about Fat Joe, they'll buy it just because it's a good product.

Studies show that African-Americans like to buy black when it authenticates what they're buying, when it puts some sort of stamp on it. That's the case across the board. If you're looking at fine apparel, for example, like a really nice suit, you'll still want to buy Italian. High-end electronics, you'll probably buy a Japanese product. Cars, maybe German. But why would I want to buy an MP3 player from a black manufacturer? What's the advantage? I definitely don't want to buy black pizza, and I don't want to buy black Chinese food. I want to buy it from a Chinese guy.

The same gap I saw for FUBU in the apparel world is the gap I now see for hundreds of different companies and brands, managed by people who need to think outside the box a little bit. It takes vision and guts and faith and all those good things, to recognize the buying power of the African-American community and discover new ways to tap into it. And it takes the shared vision of a partner with the money and resources to help you see it through. If you think it's crazy, remember that Samsung was the 8th largest company in the world, with annual sales over $80 billion, when they hooked up with four little black boys from Queens, and to date we have shipped over $5 billion. That's buying power—and selling power.

African-Americans, when we're making any kind of significant purchase, we're aspiring to something. We're buying into an ideal we have for ourselves, and we want to know we're getting the best our money can buy. It's a statement. All purchases are statement purchases, if it's not to cover a basic need, and this is especially true for African-Americans. They say we wear our wealth on our sleeves, and it's true. We absolutely do. It's a respect thing. But it's also a self-respect thing, which means we need to stop beating ourselves up over this and making each and every purchase as if the health of our community depended on it. Some of us, we just want to know we got a good deal. End of story.

The time when manufacturers and marketers could pimp their way around the marketplace and dictate to the crowd is long gone. Now the power has shifted. Now the crowd dictates to the manufacturer, and the business of buying and selling has been tilted every which way—most of which cross all cultural lines and break every known barrier to entry in most consumer-based industries. There's no more, *Make it and they will come*. The consumer drives the product, and I take this as a great good thing. It makes it an exciting time to be marketing goods and services to the American consumer, and at FUBU I think we've done well to stay out in front of these changes. Anyway, we've meant to. Are we market visionaries? Not at all. Do we get it right every time out? No way. Hell, we've messed up more times than I can remember, and misread our market in ways that cost us a lot of money, but for the most part we've kept in step with our core consumer.

The main thing is, we've tried to bend and tilt with the times. That's been our mission ever since we opened up shop. I tend to date our success at FUBU back to those very first tie-top hats, Easter weekend, 1991, so we've been at this a good long while, which means there's been a lot of bending and tilting. We've seen our initial target market age out of our initial line, but we've aged right alongside, to where we now offer all kinds of products that carry the FUBU name. Some of them we make ourselves, and some of them we license out, to extend our reach. At FUBU, we were never *just* about t-shirts and tie-top hats, but over the years, thanks to the brand-extending power of various licensing deals, we've been about shoes, boots, bags, lingerie, hair care products, formal wear, watches, fragrances, eyewear, a children's line, a women's line, and on and on.

Honestly, I never gave any of these licensing opportunities a thought when we were starting out. It was so far from my thinking I didn't even know such opportunities existed. But I came to realize it's like found money, and a great way to grow your brand without busting your butt. If some company wanted to do business with us, if they wanted to capitalize on our successful brand and the market penetration that presumably came along with it, then we were all for it. If you came to us with a reasonable plan, one that didn't poach on our core business or cheapen the FUBU name, and if it seemed to us you could deliver on it, there was a good chance we'd sign on and see what happened. What did we have to lose, right? We took the same approach as we expanded into free-standing storefront operations, in the United States and abroad. If it made sense, we went for it; if it seemed like a stretch, we let it go.

It's hit-or-miss with these tie-ins, and it changes each season. For example, our watch company partners went out of business right after they launched our line. We signed R. Kelly to do a gorgeous campaign to promote our new fragrance line, and then had to scrap the whole thing when we learned he was about to be investigated on criminal charges. Sometimes, the companies we were doing business with couldn't make good on payments due us, and we had to take legal action to collect our fair share. Sometimes, they underestimated demand and couldn't make good on their orders, leaving the FUBU name a little bit tarnished by association. There were even some growing pains with Jordache, the company that made the first "designer" jeans, which put out our women's line, as we figured how to take some of the hard edges of the FUBU look and soften them up for the fairer sex. Turned out our Jordache partners knew their stuff, and they ended up teaching us a few things about the industry—reminding me yet again that you should never be so arrogant or full of yourself to think you know it all, even when you're riding high. (*Especially* when you're riding high!)

But we had our share of positive associations as well. Thanks to our free-standing stores in these markets, FUBU became the number one selling brand in Korea and France. We're even in Saudi Arabia, of all places. One year, we had the best-selling line of bedding at Bed, Bath & Beyond, and one of the top selling tuxedos in the country, so you never know when one of these things is really going to take off—and when it does, it's good news all around. Good for the licensee. Good for the licensor. Good, even for our flagship customers, because it contributes to our bottom line and allows us to keep costs down in other areas.

>> SMELLS LIKE HIP-HOP

A word or two on our aborted attempt to get into the fragrance business. Russell Simmons had tried to penetrate this market about a year ahead of FUBU, and he met big resistance from retailers who kept telling him they didn't buy hip-hop fragrances. Don't know how you can smell hip-hop, but this was the reception he received. Still, he went ahead and created a beautiful bottle and a nice fragrance, only there were some problems with the design. The bottles tended to break in shipping, which was about the last thing he needed when he was launching a new line. He'd already been met with all this resistance, and once he started having trouble with the packaging he was derailed.

We stepped in the following year with a fragrance of our own, Plush, and the resistance was still there. We were working with an established fragrance company, but still we kept hearing, "We're not gonna let you guys into the fragrance market." And now they could point to their bad experience with Russell as one of their reasons. After all, it stood to reason to these retailers that if one hip-hop fragrance had some trouble then another would be in line for more of the same. But we went ahead with our plans, and developed a nice fragrance and some compelling packaging. We were good to go. We shot a beautiful ad campaign with R. Kelly and Rosalyn Sanchez, but we never got to run those ads because of that looming R. Kelly controversy. We had to eat that whole shoot.

Nevertheless, we sent the fragrance out to a couple stores and started to do really well with it, even without a supporting ad campaign, but after a while sales started to flatten—primarily because most retailers felt the product wasn't right for them at the moment. Plush was meant to evoke a certain level of success, and comfort, and accomplishment. That was the idea behind the campaign we never got to run. But there was still the notion out there that a black or hip-hop fragrance wouldn't work, and ultimately we had to pull the plug on the project because we weren't getting anywhere with it.

But the reach and power of the mavens of the urban market is like the bird flu, I've come to realize. You've got all these designers and manufacturers trying to figure out that virus, trying to get into the human strain, and these efforts are regenerating and gaining strength and power and momentum, and sooner or later someone will come in and unlock that market and the virus will spread like crazy. In the end, that's what happened here. My boy Puffy came out with a fragrance called "Unforgivable," and it ended up as the number one selling fragrance in history. And this was just three years after Russell Simmons got all that flack about people not wanting to buy a hip-hop fragrance. Russell took his swing at it. We took our swing at it. And then finally Puffy knocked it down. Now the doors are wide open.

One of the great things about our success with FUBU was that people took notice. Wasn't just our licensing partners. Wasn't just that each season we managed to sell through our lines and generate enough heat to carry us over into the next season. Wasn't just that we somehow managed to build FUBU into a lifestyle brand, a line that seemed to symbolize a certain kind of success, a certain way of expressing yourself, a certain way of looking back at the world. We weren't the first urban designers on the scene, and as long as I'm on it let me just say that I've often cringed at the label, even though I use it myself. Exactly what makes our clothes *urban*? Is it that black people are wearing them? We used to wear Timberlands and Le Coq Sportif, but nobody ever called them urban lines. Is it because we're designing them? There were black designers at Adidas and Polo, but they were working behind the scenes. Is it because we're black-owned? I guess this has to be it, even though there were black-owned companies in other industries that never had to shoulder the term. I mean, can you imagine a black defense attorney going partners with another black defense attorney and having some reporter label their practice *urban*? Even worse, *hip-hop*?

Whatever you called us, we pioneered a whole segment of the fashion industry, and our sales soared. With each monetary success there was also a tremendous sense of validation, which we could measure by the line forming of people wanting to pick our brains. Early on, I started getting all kinds of phone calls, from this and that corporate executive, wanting to know if I could help him or her tap into the youth market in their arena. Not to blow smoke up my own butt or anything, but I became a fairly sought after consultant in certain circles, because there weren't many other entrepreneurs or executives as in touch with the urban market. White companies, black companies . . . every-color-of-the-rainbow companies. They could see that we were plugged in to our consumer in ways they couldn't imagine, so they reached out. I even went out on the speaking circuit, appearing at colleges like Brandeis University, and before venture capitalist conventions and large corporations, speaking about the power of the urban market.

This got to be a fairly interesting side job for the way it introduced me to any number of new opportunities. At one point, I met Larry Miller, who was the head guy at Brand Jordan, over at Nike. We ended up becoming good friends, but at the time I guess you could say we were in play. We were talking to a lot of people, about all kinds of deals and associations, and in the back of my head I was thinking there might be a way to bring me and my boys onto the Nike campus and extend our penetration through their marketing. At least it was worth a conversation, so Larry invited me to an executive conference he was running in New York, with about twenty of his top people, and I gave them my two cents on what I thought Nike was doing right in the marketplace, and where they were coming up short.

Now, I had to have been pretty full of myself to tell a company like Nike what they should be doing, because the truth of the matter is they've got it on lock. Hands down, they're the number one company on the planet in terms of branding and imaging, but in my opinion they've got too much attention focused in just one area. Sports, that's their main thing, and my take is, if they can make $15 billion by associating their brand with athletes, maybe they can push it to $18 or $19 billion if they sign on a select group of actors, musicians, designers, businessmen . . . people who represent something meaningful to potential customers who aren't looking to athletes as role models, people who aren't athletes themselves. After all, don't they *just do it* as well? Nike sells tons of merchandise to people who haven't broken a sweat since high school—walking-around shoes, comfortable sweats and training suits, whatever the case may be. Call it lifestyle clothing, or freestyle clothing, or whatever you want, but it's a different market than their athletic clothing, a whole different deal. Wouldn't it make sense to sign a musical artist, and let his or her star power rub off on the Nike swoosh, so that all these non-athletes might have someone to emulate?

This one meeting with Larry and his group went so well he invited me out to the Nike complex to present to the company's top brass. Their headquarters were just incredible. Swimming pools, tennis courts, tracks, full gyms . . . it was almost like a college campus, except a couple times bigger. I was told that at any time of day Nike employees could leave their desks to go work out, and I thought, What a way to run a company! But it works. It seemed like every top executive short of Phil Knight himself was in the room to hear my pitch, and I went at it again. I explained how they needed to think outside the sports box, and pay attention to what some of their competitors were doing, like the people over at Reebok. Reebok had been dead-in-the-water just a couple years earlier, and then they signed Jay-Z and 50 Cent and all these other artists, and their market share started to climb. These guys weren't just endorsing the brand—they had their own shoes, their own clothing line, whatever. And you could chart the spike in Reebok's sales and draw a direct line to this push in entertainment. I told these Nike guys there are only so many Michael Jordans, only so many Tiger Woodses. These kinds of superstar athletes come around only once a generation. But in the entertainment world, there are dozens and dozens of artists who receive the same kind of adulation and respect from their fans, whose endorsement could translate to sales, as long as that artist remained hot.

I broke it down. I said, "Michael Jordan is one player. He might be the focus, the center of attention in the games he plays, but he's not the only player people are looking at. He's on a court with nine other guys, for about two hours, about 80 nights a year. His games are broadcast on a specific channel, written up in a specific section of the paper, and for about half the year you don't see him at all. And if you don't care about basketball, you can miss out on his comings and goings entirely."

Then I compared the reach of a guy like Jordan to someone like Jay-Z. I said, "When Jay-Z gives a concert, he's the only guy on the court. Everyone is just looking at him. His videos run three and a half minutes, but they're played over and over, on MTV, BET, VH1, MuchMusic and dozens of other channels. They're played in clubs. And his songs reinforce those images from his videos every time they're played on the radio. Even if you don't buy his albums, or go out to the clubs, or watch music video channels, it's hard to escape his music. It's in the air, and all around. And he's not just about one thing, like basketball. He's all over the place. He's dictating to kids his opinions on various matters, the type of lifestyle they should be pursuing, what they should be wearing, drinking, eating, driving, whatever. If he talks about a new style or a product in one of his songs, it's validated in the minds of millions of his fans. If he wears a hot new line of clothes in one of his videos, it's like the ultimate product placement."

>> THE NIGGA THIS YEAR

I have a theory, and I've tried to work against it as I've attempted to grow our brand. It goes like this: there's only enough room for one black guy at a time. I don't buy it, and I certainly don't like it, but historically that's how it's gone—at least that's how it's gone in the fashion business. When you're coming up, you'll get your shot. You'll get some floor space and sell some pieces. You'll be the token black guy for a while, but as soon as you're out of style they'll make way for the next guy. It's like it's a one-at-a-time deal, and we're supposed to take turns.

My boy Keith Clinkscale, when he was president of *Vibe* magazine, used to tell me he'd get calls at least once a week from haters wanting him to do a story on FUBU because they heard we weren't black-owned. Or maybe the calls came from our competition, wanting to put salt in our game for whatever reason. It's almost funny, the reports we heard from media-types like Keith, that people were calling us JEW-BU instead of FUBU, because of our association with the Weisfeld family.

People were lining up to cut us down. You don't see that in other industries. Go to the jewelry district, on 47th Street. You've got all these guys working together, in unity, supporting each other. If one of them does well, they all do well, because there's a spillover effect. But if the "Nigga This Year" is only given this one little area in the department store, if you're the only line there, if you don't have a bunch of supporting lines to create a whole "urban" or streetwear department, you'll be out of that store the next season. That's why I've tried to embrace all these other lines that have launched in

FUBU's wake. Jay-Z's RocaWear. Puffy's Sean Jean. Russell Simmons's Phat Farm. As one does well, we all do well. Across the board. A lot of people think I'm crazy, to help these guys and support them when they're trying to compete for my business, but I believe it keeps us out in front. These are the type of people, you're not about to keep them from being successful. You can help them or not, but you can't stand in their way.

Back to my Nike visit and the cross-over power of some of these entertainment artists. They're covered in countless newspapers and magazines and on-line 'zines, and not just in one section like the sports section. They're working every day of the year, not just six months. They might come up as a rapper, but soon enough they're actors, and producers, and music video directors. They're everywhere. They're promoting a new album, or an upcoming concert, or a new video, not to mention the coverage you get from the albums, concerts and videos themselves. Really, there's a kind of wall-to-wall exposure that can be far greater than what they could get out of a single Michael Jordan—taking nothing away from MJ, who's the greatest. A rapper with a hot new single, he's getting six to seven thousand spins each week on radio stations across the country. Even a halfway decent song gets three to four thousand spins, and if it's a hit . . . well, then you can just forget about it. Our kids will be singing a Jay-Z song for the next five years, reinforcing whatever brand he's associated with each time out, and he puts out three or four singles per album, so it all adds up.

I said, "It's great to go out and sign the Super Bowl MVP, but who will even remember this guy when the next football season rolls around? Plus, there's only one Super Bowl MVP, right? There are dozens and dozens of hot new artists each season. That makes it easier to sign any given one of them, at a price that makes sense."

At the time of our meeting on the Nike campus, Reebok was on its way up, making its push, and I told these guys to keep their eyes on them. Turned out Adidas was watching, too, because they ended up buying Reebok the following year, for $3.8 billion—making them the second-largest shoe company in the world and slowly creeping up on Nike. I hadn't been encouraging these Nike guys to break their mold, or even to look over their shoulders and pay attention to their competition. I mean, they'd had ridiculous success, doing what they were doing, and I had no doubt they would continue having that ridiculous success. But I was suggesting that they expand that mold a little bit. If they put out a thousand styles of shoes each year, why not have fifty "lifestyle" shoes, aligned with certain artists? Why not dip their toes into these waters and gauge the temperature? It was all about scale, and taking retail space from their competitors.

They could have hooked up with FUBU and used our influence to tap into the hip-hop world, but I don't think they heard me. Or maybe they did and figured they could go this route on their own, but I had given my opinion, and I share it here because we'll all do well to think beyond whatever ceiling we've put over our heads. Going forward, you can bet you'll see companies aligning with entertainment artists more and more. Doesn't mean they'll be signing less athletes, but they'll start to spread those dollars around, across the pop culture spectrum. It makes good business sense. It's a huge potential market, when you think about all the different ways you can be bombarded with a hit song. How many times it's played on the radio, how many times the video is played, how many times it plays in the clubs, or in mix-tapes, or downloads. It could be eight to ten thousand times a week, you have some guy singing about his S.Carter shoes, and you have to think this is way more effective than throwing in with a single athlete, no matter how great or legendary that athlete might be. These artists, they won't get injured and miss a season. They're a safe bet. True, the rap on some of these hip-hop guys is they're always getting shot, but even that can work in your favor, in terms of brand association. I don't mean to sound harsh or flip, but Tupac sold more albums dead than alive—over 50 million units!—making him the second-hottest selling deceased artist after Elvis, so it won't kill you.

>> HEY, HEY, HEY

I'll share a licensing story, to give some idea how these deals usually go and to reinforce my belief that you get back in business what you put into it. Back in the late 1990s, there was a company called Iceberg that had a high-end line of fine-knit sweaters, pants and shirts with a whole mess of licensed characters on them. Snoopy. Bart Simpson. Like that. Some of these sweaters would sell for $600, and I thought we could do better with the same concept at a more affordable price so I reached out to Bill Cosby and inquired about the Fat Albert and the Cosby Kids license, which was all but dormant at the time. Me and my boys had grown up on these characters, and I thought we might tap into people's nostalgia and do well with them, in this context. Later on, we'd branch out to other licensed characters, like the animated Harlem Globetrotters, but Fat Albert was our first and most successful tie-in with these sweaters, which we marketed under our Platinum FUBU line.

The upshot to this one is that our sweaters did better than we could have expected, priced about

40 percent less—and in the end Platinum FUBU killed the Iceberg line. We also put Fat Albert back on the map, reviving interest to where there'd soon be a live-action movie built around a line that had basically been on the shelf. All this happened in the stretch of three or four years, and in all that time I never dealt with Bill Cosby personally. It was just lawyers talking to lawyers, but we must have sent him $10 million or so in licensing fees, and I found it a little surprising that he didn't even send a note of thanks. Just a note. I mean, someone helps you earn all that money and jump-start an asset that really wasn't doing all that much, you'd think a thank you note was in order, right? I didn't have to license Fat Albert. I could have gone after Underdog. Manny Jackson, the owner of the Globetrotters, a very respected, successful businessman in his own right, he made some money on the line and made it a point to come up to our offices to thank us for the opportunity. Muhammad Ali, we also put his likeness on some of these items, and he made a good chunk on his end, and even he came up in his condition to show his appreciation. This is a man who once had the third most recognizable face in the world, behind Mickey Mouse and the Pope, so this was huge. When he left our building, and word had gotten around that he was inside, there were hundreds of people gathered in front of the Empire State Building, waiting for him to come back out. And as a result of that meeting I ended

up befriending Ali's manager, Bernie Yuman, who now acts as my manager as well.

Most businesses are built on relationships. It's how you treat people that counts. I don't have a beef with Bill Cosby over this, because business is business. But I've got to tell you, I didn't go out of my way to keep that Fat Albert line going, once the terms ran out. Each side had done well, but that was the end of it, and when the dust cleared I realized how important it is to show a little love in this kind of situation. And I've made sure ever since, whenever somebody licenses the FUBU name, I always call over and thank them for wanting to get into business with us in the first place. I'm very grateful, because they're putting money in my pocket, and I don't care how rich or how successful you are, or how deep your pockets have become, there's always room for a little more money in there.

It's one thing to wave your own flag, but to have someone else put their money, their expertise and their sweat into your dreams, in this dog-eat-dog world . . . it's an honor.

I want to go back to that "One Less Shrimp" analogy from a couple chapters back, that all-important lesson I learned while I was working at Red Lobster, about how it's the little things that add up. There was a best-selling book not too long ago that said, "Don't Sweat the Small Stuff," but for my money that's exactly what you need to do if you mean to stand out. It's the small stuff that makes the biggest difference when it comes to establishing a brand—and the big picture that comes into focus only after the details have been covered. At FUBU, that meant the little things we did to make our product stand out. We couldn't put three sleeves on our shirts but we paid attention to details. We used the finest materials, the heaviest fabrics, the best zippers and buttons. We personally serviced our accounts. We went big into embroidery, when our competitors were still silk-screening or heat-sealing, and a lot of our highlights were hand-sewn. These small things added up, as people came to associate our brand with quality.

Truth is, everything you do in business adds up, just as every little misstep can cost you. I've tried to keep this in mind, all along. At FUBU, for example, we never went in for those big advertising campaigns, putting all our eggs in one basket, preferring instead to spread our ad dollars around. First of all, we did all our advertising in-house, so that was one way to keep our costs down (and to keep the look of our company in line with our vision). But then if I had a million dollars to spend to promote our line, I'd put it to work ten times instead of one, put it into one video, one song, one print ad, one club campaign . . . and we'd get a bigger run for our money.

Wasn't just advertising, where we played it small and close to the vest. In areas like marketing, too, we tended to go the easiest, most obvious route. *Keep it Simple, Stupid.* That's the old buzzword in marketing and advertising—KISS—and my thing was to keep it real simple. When it came to focus group testing, we were like the guy who owns Arizona Iced Tea. His idea of a focus group was to lay in his company's new products in his refrigerator at home. Whatever drinks his kids reached for most often, that's what they went with. We took the same approach. We'd design, design, design, make as many samples as we could. Then we'd put them in our showroom and see which items our own people wanted to steal from the racks. All our guys wear our clothes, and if I kept hearing, "Daymond, I want that piece," I knew we had something going for us.

But most CEOs don't operate in this kind of hands-on way, not anymore. They don't think for themselves. You've got these big companies all split up into so many different layers, they're insulated from what's going on. They're afraid to take chances, even thought that's how they got to where they are in the first place, by taking chances. But you can't get too comfortable, too complacent. You can't lose touch. You have to check out a guy like Rupert Murdoch, who recently bought a big stake in MySpace, a cutting edge portal that's hard-wired into every teenager's computer, and remind yourself that you can never get too set in your ways. Chris Latimer, the guy who turned me on to those hockey jerseys when we were first getting started, who's gone on to be enormously influential as an event planner and image consultant, he still comes up to my office every couple months and says, "Okay, Daymond, time to get you out of your ivory tower. We're gonna go to some clubs, and we're gonna go to the 'hood, and we're gonna hang out and touch everybody and see where you're at." Every time I'm in the 'hood it's a valuable lesson. It helps me to know where the needle is, and whether or not our message is getting out there the way we want it out there. I'll go into a club, someone will spot me as one of the FUBU guys, he'll come up to me and say, "Last year you made this one piece, I loved it. I can't wait for you to do another one like that." Or I'll hear, "What the hell happened to you guys? You made something hot last year, and this year there's nothing. What's wrong with you?"

Either way, I love it, because it keeps me connected. Tells me what we're doing right, what we're doing wrong, what we need to fix. And it puts it out there that we're still a part of the community we mean to serve. We're not so big that we can't party with our customers—that sounds like the Cristal guy, if you ask me.

>> HANDS ON

I'm a big fan of any corporate executive who manages to keep in close and constant touch with his customers, or who undertakes any initiative to help him do so, and I'll shine a light on one here. I was at an awards ceremony not too long ago with David Neeleman, CEO of JetBlue, which is probably one of the few airlines making any kind of money these days. If you've ever taken one of their flights, you'll know they do things a little differently over there. They pump up the whole travel experience, and make it fun—and affordable. It's a winning formula, and a real departure from the cold, impersonal way the major carriers do their thing.

Anyway, JetBlue had just beaten us out as Ernst & Young's Entrepreneurs of the Year, and I hung out with David Neeleman and JetBlue's President and COO David Barger at the event to announce the awards. We'd already won the regional award, so I didn't mind when we lost out to JetBlue on the national award, especially to a company that managed to make some serious noise in an industry that has long been one of the toughest to crack.

Neeleman's secret to staying on top of his business? Along with his colleague Barger, he makes it a point to ride at least one of his flights each week. Simple enough, right? And they don't just sit back and relax and enjoy the ride. They work the ticket counter, handle the baggage, hand out snacks,

> fluff pillows, walk the aisle and talk to customers. In this way, these guys get to know their business inside out and upside down. They keep in touch, and get their hands dirty, and I have to think this is one of the main reasons why JetBlue has given the big boys at American Airlines, Delta and Continental all kinds of fits in their first few years of operation. They're lean and hungry and smart enough to put themselves on the line—literally.

I always thought there was tremendous advantage in staying small. The small guy, the stealth guy will always find a way in to any market. Once a company gets too big, it's afraid to take chances. In a big, lumbering corporate environment, you can't respond quickly to a sudden change in the marketplace, or roll out a new line of clothing to capitalize on new trend. It takes much more energy to move in a new direction, to respond to a sudden shift, to change your stripes in any kind of meaningful way. That's why my friend Keith Clinkscale, former president and CEO of *Vibe* magazine, talks about these giant companies being blind-sided by their upstart competitors. The big bookstore chains didn't see Amazon coming. Xerox didn't see Canon coming. IBM didn't see Microsoft coming. ABC, CBS and NBC didn't see Fox coming—and for what it's worth, let's remember that Fox launched on the back of mostly black programming like "Roc" and "In Living Color." Nobody saw Google coming. And, in some ways, Nike didn't see Reebok coming.

The small guys will always find a way to win, and they'll be able to shift on the fly and adapt, and the lesson here is not just to keep your company in fighting trim but to keep your eyes in the rear-view mirror and your side-view mirrors and at the same time on the road ahead—not the easiest thing to do when you're driving a massive 18-wheeler. Agility, that's the key. Big companies can't respond as swiftly as their smaller competitors because there are too many layers, too much bureaucracy, and that's no way to be. Opportunities turn up, and you have to be able to rise to meet them. Sometimes I have to be able to get somebody to a video set in California by seven o'clock the next morning. Magazines have an open page, at a reduced rate, and you need to be able to jump on that before they go to press. Or maybe a store owner will call and tell you so-and-so didn't make his delivery and you need to ship 10,000 pieces within a month to get the order. You need to have an infrastructure in place that will allow you to get these unexpected things done, but more than that you need people to actually do them. At FUBU, sometimes that person will be me. I'll hop on the plane. I'll show up on the set. If I need to, I'll order a bunch of blank t-shirts from somewhere and send them out to a local embroiderer to get the job done. I have to have that agility. I even went to film school, to study what goes on during these video and commercial shoots, so I'll know what to expect when I get there. The bigger you are, the more cumbersome you are, the less likely you'll be able to do that. Big companies can't do that. FUBU can.

Small is the new big, especially in the fashion industry. Don't get me wrong, big accounts are fine, and in many respects they're necessary to your overall success as a company, but when your line is only carried at Macy's, let's say, there's no interaction between the company and the consumer. Not only that, there's a giant institution—a department store chain!—standing between you and any relationship you might have with your customer. It's impersonal. The kid working the floor doesn't feel any kind of connection to your product. He doesn't even feel a connection to the people on the floor. He doesn't care which items he sells, as long as he sells. But if you're also in a boutique-type store, you've got people working for you. It's personal. You've got a small store owner who's plugged in to what's hot and new. He wants to build a level of trust with his customers, so they'll come back to his store and look to him for advice on what to wear, so they'll buy from him instead of from the big department stores. He can say, "Hey, check out this new line." Or, he can bury you. He can say, "They've gotten too big, their quality is going downhill," and when that happens a thousand times around the country it can eliminate your brand. You want to cater to these guys so they'll talk you up, and take a rooting interest in your success, almost like they have a stake in it—which, in a way, they do, because the more pieces they sell the better terms we can offer on their next order, which means there'll be more money flowing their way.

I know a mother and daughter team in Florida that owns a fairly successful Coral Gables boutique called Aura, and they're always telling me how important it is to have "window-shoppers" come in to their store who can't really afford their merchandise, or who just don't want to buy at the time. It's gotten so they can spot these people a mile away, just by their body language. They don't ignore these customers, the way some other store owners might. Instead, they make them feel comfortable, encourage them to try on a couple items, leave them feeling like they want to save up some money and come back to make a purchase. They'll talk up the hot new lines to these people, and send them home with something to shoot for, something to think about, and even though there's no "transaction" taking place in any kind of traditional sense, it's all part of business. It's the power to see past the immediate dollar to the long-term benefit, and if I'm a clothing manufacturer I want someone like these women hand-selling my pieces. And it's not just at Aura, where you find this mindset. You see it from my boy Izzy at "Up Against the Wall," and Gil at "Trends," and a handful of other boutique retailers.

In "The Tipping Point," Malcolm Gladwell talks about the so-called "mavens of the market," the people who cast themselves as helpers in the marketplace. We all know someone like this, someone who stays on top of each trend, someone who knows the best place to buy the best new clothes at the best prices. It doesn't have to be clothes—it can be housewares or antiques or electronics—but I'll stick to what I know. These people might not have the money to buy the clothes themselves, but they get a certain high from turning other people on to what they know. They like the authority that comes with their inside insights. They like that their friends look to them for tips on what to buy.

Gladwell suggests that these types of consumers should be courted and encouraged to spend time in your store, and I'll take it to the next level and suggest that when you're building a style-conscious, status-conscious brand you need as many window-shoppers as you can get. Not mavens, necessarily, but just plain people who might be your target consumer but for the fact that they don't have the money to buy in just yet. Or maybe they're not ready to buy just yet. For now, these are customers in only the loosest sense, but they just want to check you out and soak in the experience and file it away for later. They're the ones who'll aspire to your line, and they're the ones who'll spread the word about your line to their friends and colleagues sooner than the customers who are actually buying the stuff. Those high-end shoppers, the ones who can afford to buy whatever they want, they're not so quick to tell their friends where they got this or that hot new outfit because they don't want their friends looking just like them. They want to stand out—or, to stand apart. But the small-frys, the shrimps, the *just-lookers* . . . they'll talk you up. And as soon as they have enough money in their pockets, they'll be back to buy that piece they've had their eye on all this time.

>> CHANGE IT UP

At FUBU, if we didn't shift with our market, we'd be on the scrap heap, but we were able to anticipate the changing needs of our core consumer and make some adjustments. Same goes for every successful brand on the American corporate landscape. Look at a brand like Listerine, which started out as a house-cleaning product. All of a sudden, they figured out a diluted version of the stuff would work on the germs in your mouth. They came up with a slogan, talking about how Listerine kills chronic halitosis, at a time when no one in the country even knew what the term meant. Nobody talked about bad breath. It just existed. Now, 100 years later, they've got products that melt on your tongue, they've got sprays, they've got all kinds of different dispensers. They've kept reinventing themselves, and they're still a vibrant and viable line, and if these guys can grow a floor cleaning product into a mouthwash empire then brand extension is within every company's reach. And it should be every company's priority. A friend of mine once told me that the only company that doesn't need to market or refocus its line is the U.S. Treasury Department, and I take his point.

Walk up and down any aisle in the grocery store, and you'll see versions of that Listerine transformation played out in a lot of different ways. Ketchup, toothpaste, snack foods . . . all these companies, building on their established brands to make sure the consumer doesn't leave them behind. Candy companies, like M&M Mars, coming up with all kinds of ways to sell the same chocolate. M&M minis, special colors, cookies, candy bars . . . They've even got M&M dolls and figurines. They've turned it into a movement, and if you can do that with a fistful of candies that melt in your mouth and not in your hands, you can do it with anything.

Too many times, you get these CEOs behind their big desks, counting their money, and counting on their company's reputation to make them piles more, but if they don't put in the time and effort and creative energy to vitalize their brands and keep them contemporary, they'll melt in your hands before they get anywhere near your mouth. And if they can't put in the time and effort themselves, they can reach out to an outside consultant or specialist, someone with experience in this type of approach.

I've tried to keep myself and my clothing brands relevant by also changing it up. In the past, I've directed many of our in-house videos and commercials, but I've lately turned to directing music artists like Fat Joe as well. I became a real student of the form, hanging around as many video sets as I could, to soak up what I could. And when it came time to direct my first video, I surrounded myself with the best. Eric White, Jesse Terrero, Dr. Teeth, Benny Boom, Chris Robinson and of course my childhood friend Hype Williams, the hands-down creator of this space.

Don't be so set in your ways that you fail to recognize how a shift or a trend in another arena might impact your bottom line. Let's call it the Sudoku effect. You've seen those Japanese numbers puzzles, right? They're carried in every newspaper in the country, and Sudoku books have been a boon to paperback publishers and on-line game sites that have been quick to capitalize on their popularity. But did you know that in 2005, the first full year the Sudoku craze was in effect in this country, sales of Number 2 pencils increased by over 700%. And who do you think made money on that sideline surge? It was the savvy CEO with his eyes open wide enough to see that all these Sudoku nuts would need pencils to complete their puzzles, and to make sure his factory was prepared to meet the sudden demand.

The way we decided to grow at FUBU was to take on other brands that would not cannibalize our core business. The thinking was to establish all these different anchors for our company, and give us every opportunity to reach out to every type of consumer. Anchors, tent-poles, divisions . . . doesn't matter what you call them, for us they're really just a way to diversify our assets and spread our costs (and risks) over several different lines, the same way an NFL coach comes up with a bunch of different options in the team playbook. Once we got up to a healthy level with our signature line, we started to strike distribution deals with lines like Willie Esco, Kappa/USA and Drunken Munky. These labels had their core following—in the Latino market, in the athletic market and among skateboarder types—so we figured since they didn't poach on our existing market we'd do well to partnering with them.

And we did—almost right away. In fact, we did so well with these established lines, we soon looked to acquire another label outright. Specifically, we looked to an Australian company called Coogi, which had been around since 1969. They'd hit their high-water mark in the 1980s with a colorful line of sweaters made popular by Bill Cosby on the hit NBC series "The Cosby Show." Most of their stuff sold for about $700, and back then I didn't know too many people who could afford to spend that much money on a single item, but the line did well, until the mid 1990s or so when they ran out of steam. I thought there was an opportunity here for us to establish a luxury label to sit on top of our signature FUBU line, so we bought the company and pumped up the name and started putting our stamp on a whole new line aimed at our core, inner-city, trend-setting market—people with a little more money in their pockets to spend on high-end pieces that might be a little more suitable to wear to work or to a fashionable club.

We also went out and struck a partnership deal with Heatherette, a white-hot women's line put out by the designers Richie Rich and Traver Rains. These guys were club kids, through and through, and they had the whole club scene wired to promote their line. Paris Hilton, Courtney Love, Pamela Anderson, Naomi Campbell . . . they had all these celebrities, coming and going, clamoring for their clothes. Photographers like David LaChapelle would shoot their ads for free, because Richie and Traver were such charismatic, interesting people, and because their clothes were just hotter than hot. They reminded me of me, the way they hustled, the way they refused to take no for an answer, the way they courted the press and kept plugged in to their world, the way they believed in their designs and did whatever it took to stand out, so it was almost inevitable that we would hook up. As it happened, we sought each other out, and both sides knew there was a deal to be made, and now we're proud to have Heatherette as part of the FUBU family.

The cutting edge keeps changing. What's hot one season is cool the next, and what's daring one year is tame twelve months later. Someone keeps moving the line on us, and at FUBU we've tried to anticipate those changes. We've used these other clothing lines to help us reposition ourselves from one season to the next, to stay out in front, and along the way we've introduced some new lines to reinforce what we do best—namely, to create a kind of movie around a clothing line, an image, and stay out of the way. Other designers fall in love with their name, but we've taken a backseat on these newer lines, and one of my favorite things is when someone comes up to me at a club wearing Coogi, saying "FUBU's wack," or "FUBU's dead," and meanwhile they're still wearing our stuff. They don't know it, but they're still wearing my clothes, and I just laugh to myself. That's what keeps us vibrant and fresh. The brand names, they get a little stale after a while, so you need these reinforcements.

We've had to push the edges a bit with each new line. FUBU was raw for its time, but the more successful we became, the more prominent we became, the more we lost that edge. Look at it this way: Redd Foxx was raw for his time, until Richard Pryor came along, and he looked tame next to Eddie Murphy, who in turn looked tame next to Dave Chappelle. You ratchet it up, each time out, but you can't go back. You can't backpedal. Once FUBU has reached into the middle America department stores, we can't give back that ground, but at the same time we don't want to give up our edge, so we keep coming out with harder and harder designs, to recast our core customer. Just recently, we've backed a line called Ether that's about as raw and edgy as anything on the market, and you can bet that if we tried to get any of those items into Macy's we'd be shown the door.

You have to stay out in front of demand, create new demand, cater to your hardcore customers who look to you to help them determine what's hot, what's new, what they should be buying. The people at Mercedes Benz have been able to do that by introducing the Maybach, and the 500 and 600 series, super high-end luxury cars that are out of reach even for most Mercedes customers. Ralph Lauren has been able to do it, with specialty stores and couture lines and special edition lines. Disney has been able to do it, by creating a false sense of demand for its DVD titles, pulling them off the market and reintroducing them several years later.

And we've tried to change it up at FUBU as well—by launching FUBU Platinum, or repositioning the Coogi line, or just infusing a different kind of energy into our public image. When our early ad campaign got a little tired, to give just one example, we went out and hired the model Tyson Beckford, straight off his exclusive Polo campaign. You've all seen this guy. He'd been the ubiquitous Polo model for years and years, and soon as he came out of that deal he signed on with us. We had all these ad agency types telling us he might be too closely associated with the Polo line to bring any carry-over benefit to FUBU, but I never listened to these guys. (Those are the same kind of fools who didn't even know who I was when they were in my office!) I just liked the fact that Tyson was so closely aligned with one of the world's best brands, and that we had enough strength and money and cache for him to consider coming over to work with us. He liked our brand. He got with his manager, Beth Ann Hardison (Kadeem's mother, and one of the first supermodels back in her day) and together they had the vision and understanding to work with us, while we had the guts to go against conventional wisdom and make him the face of FUBU for this one campaign.

That's how you get and keep ahead, by following your gut. Of course, it's not just your gut that takes you to your bottom line. There are certain established truths you have to pay attention to as well—like, in the apparel business the only way to maintain the exclusivity you'll need to survive and thrive long-term is to have your own retail stores. Sooner or later, if you're in someone else's store, they'll push you back to get that new guy in, but if you have your own store, like Armani or The Gap, you trap people in your own environment. You call the shots. That's one of the reasons why Abercrombie & Fitch has had such a resurgence in popularity over the past several years, because they've expanded their owned and operated franchise stores. You go into one of these stores, it's dark, there's loud music, almost like you're walking into a club, but that's the shopping environment they've created to highlight their merchandise, and it's working, while at the same time it caters to consumers at every end of the spectrum. You can go in and buy a low-end pair of pants, or something off the sale or clearance racks, but if you've got a little bit of money you can reach for that $500 pair of jeans, or one of their exclusive items, and in this way the trendsetter, tastemaker-type customer can still feel part of the brand. They've broken the whole experience into tiers, and there's money to be made at each level.

At FUBU, we could never figure this one out here at home. Yeah, internationally, we at one point had more than 50 stores, in places like Saudi Arabia, Australia and South Africa. (In Japan alone, there were seven free-standing FUBU stores!) But here at home, we were never able to make it work. We had as many as six stores in high-end outlet malls like Woodbury Commons in upstate New York, but the numbers never seemed to work for us and we ended up abandoning that end of our business. (We still maintain about 30 international locations.) I guess in the end it's because we're not retail guys; we're not real estate guys; we're designers and marketers and trendsetters, and it might have taken us a few false steps but we eventually realized we should stick to what we know—the care and feeding of the FUBU brand. It's like I always say, "My failures have fueled my successes," and here it took dropping the ball a time or two before we could run with it.

>> THE "X" FACTOR

The thing about branding is it isn't etched in stone. A brand is a mark or an image or a perception we stamp on a product, a concept or an ideal, but it doesn't last forever. Like anything else, it needs to be nurtured and reinforced, or it will start to fade. It's man-made, and it can cost millions of dollars in advertising, promotion and marketing fees for a brand to take hold. At FUBU, it's our most valuable asset, and yet for every successful brand that manages to transcend the marketplace and become a part of the culture, there are hundreds that never fully catch on with the American consumer, and hundreds more that make a small splash before disappearing in a ripple.

It's a fluid thing, this branding business, so much so that you can even see the same brand mean something completely different from one generation to the next. Take the letter X. Wasn't that long ago that the letter stood for pornography. There was a negative taint to it, if you said something was X-rated. It meant it was dirty, hardcore, subversive. To carry the tag XXX meant you were especially dirty, hardcore, subversive. Then a novelist named Douglas Copeland came out with a book called "Generation X," about a slacker group of twentysomethings who came of age during the high-tech boon, and the association started to change. Now it wasn't quite positive, but it wasn't entirely negative; it was somewhere in between.

Next, ESPN launched the Extreme Games in

1995, and the meaning changed a little more. Soon, the X stood for Xtreme, and started showing up in a positive way on product names for deodorants, snack food and video games. (There's even a beauty product known as XTreme Lashes, and a professional football team called the Los Angeles Xtreme, which plays in the Xtreme Football League—or XFL.) All of a sudden, the XXX label symbolized an extreme taken to the extreme, and it even showed up as the title of a 2002 action flick starring Vin Diesel.

Over time, even porn moved away from the letter that was once so closely identified with the adult film industry that they were nearly synonymous. The Motion Picture Association of America dropped the X from its ratings system and began labeling adult films NC-17, to indicate that no children would be admitted under the age of 17. And that Vin Diesel movie? It was released with an MPAA rating of PG-13, just to show how far we'd moved in a couple decades.

The lesson here? X doesn't always mark the spot—but something always will. And if you mean for your product, concept or ideal to get and keep an edge, you need to mark your territory with care.

If small is the new big, then maybe we should also consider that black is the new white. Conventional, middle-of-the-road companies have been slow to recognize the purchasing power of African-Americans and the hip-hop community, but they're coming around. A couple years ago, I started keeping a clip file of endorsements and professional associations you would have never seen when I was a kid, and I'll share just a few of them here to help me make my point:

- BET founder Robert L. Johnson, who sold his cable network to Viacom and used some of the proceeds to become the majority owner of the NBA's Charlotte Bobcats franchise, forms the first mainstream movie studio principally owned and operated by African-Americans. The studio, Our Stories Films, aims to produce family-friendly movies featuring primarily African-American talent and themes and marketed to black audiences . . .

- Cadillac credits its turnaround after sluggish sales in the 80s and 90s to the popularity of its Escalade SUV among rappers and other celebrities . . .

- 50 Cent announces a strategic partnership with Apple Computers to market a line of affordable home computers to the urban market . . .

- Louis Vuitton signs producer/rapper Pharrell Williams to design a new jewelry line . . .

- Jay-Z partners with Hewlett-Packard for a series of ads promoting the H-P line of personal computers . . .

- TBS launches a broadband entertainment network called GameTap, offering video games on demand, and featuring tie-in music programming with such artists as Ice Cube, Rihanna, Da Backwudz and Chammillionaire . . .

- Queen Latifah becomes the voice of Pizza Hut, delivering the memorable tag line, "Dippin' can't be denied," and almost single-handedly revitalized the Cover Girl cosmetics line . . .

- Ralph Gilles, one of a handful of African-American car designers, comes out with Chrysler's 300C, the 2005 Car of the Year, which becomes known as the "Baby Bentley" in the 'hood . . .

The concept of aspirational purchases has been central to a lot of so-called urban spending. We spend money like we mean business, like it's going out of style, like we won't be around long enough to spend through our rolls. And yet even though we spend like crazy, we don't spend nearly as much as we claim. The rapper Jadakiss says that rappers lie in about 80 percent of their rhymes, and I'm guessing that's a lowball figure. But I take his point, which suggests that all this bling, all these fast cars and expensive clothes and luxury houses, they all add up to the kind of image these artists want to present. You look at these videos and you know that half the time the house they're living in isn't theirs. You know the car is probably on some type of product placement loan from the car company, the clothes come from guys like us when the label calls wanting to make sure their artists look good, and the jewelry is borrowed from some high-end jeweler. It's no different than when you see all these Hollywood starlets on the red carpet at the Academy Awards, wearing these ridiculous designer dresses they certainly didn't pay for, and million-dollar necklaces they've borrowed for the evening, so there's nothing really new here except that rap and hip-hop bling is a little bit louder and prouder and a little more in-your-face than what you get with more mainstream Hollywood bling.

Of course, the downside to all of the product-placement and branding that goes on in the hip-hop community is that it can work against you. Every once in a while, artists can get their fans to turn on a company because of a perceived diss to the culture, like the Cristal/Jay-Z flap I wrote about earlier, or the racist rumors about Tommy Hilfiger and Troop. It happens all the time. Pepsi had to do some scrambling of its own and pledge $3 million in charity in order to get Russell Simmons to lift a threatened boycott after the soda company dropped the rapper Ludacris as a spokesperson, following negative remarks from conservative commentator Bill O'Reilly. Ironically (or, stupidly), Pepsi ran a spot during the NBA All-Star game featuring Kobe Bryant lifting weights while the Ludacris song "Welcome to Atlanta" played in the background, confirming my theory that none of these idiots know what they're doing.

Also, it's the artists who get caught in these lies who fall off the charts. TLC, Toni Braxton, MC Hammer . . . there are a ton of artists who've had big-time success and somehow ended up in bankruptcy, and part of the reason is they were found out. I don't mean to single out these few, because there have been dozens of falls from grace, but these names spring to mind. Typically, the drop in sales and popularity follows the same downward trajectory. A guy can be rapping about his Mercedes Benz, about flying here and there on his private jet, and this and that, and then it comes out that he's living in his mother's house in Brooklyn, in the basement. Nothing wrong with living in your mother's house in Brooklyn, in the basement, but it doesn't fly if you're singing about bling. Kids today, they're not about to listen to your lies once they know they're lies.

I have to think this is all about to change. There's a whole group of rappers out there who don't dwell on these types of material things. They're known as backpack rappers. Kanye West. Common. The Roots. Mos Def. Eminem. They rap about the culture, not about things. They might drop a brand name every once in a while, but it's usually about *not* having this, *not* having that. There's a great line in that Kanye West song, "All Falls Down," where he talks about some girl who couldn't afford a car so she named her daughter Alexis. (Get it? A Lexus?)

He goes on: "Then I spent 400 bucks on this, just to be like, *Nigga, you ain't up on this*/The people highest up got the lowest self-esteem/The prettiest people do the ugliest things/We shine because they hate us, trying to buy back our 40 acres/Even if you in a Benz you still a nigga in a coupe/We buy our way out of jail, but we can't buy freedom/Things we buy to cover up inside/Drug dealers buy Jordans, crackheads buy crack, and the white man get paid off all a that . . . "

>> WHO'S IN YOUR EAR?

When I consult with other CEOs and corporate leaders, one of the first things I ask is where they're getting their ideas. Who's advising them? Is it their advertising agency? The people who have a vested interest in getting them to run a big campaign, because the bigger the campaign the bigger the vig, which can run to over twenty percent? Their brand manager? Some guy who's interested in jobbing out the budget you've prepared for him to vendors who'll give him Knicks tickets or smoked hams or luxury vacations? Their Chief Marketing Officer, who can't honestly claim to know every aspect of every market? (Just as a side note, did you know that the average lifespan of a CMO is 24 months?) Chances are the CMO doesn't even know the best person to talk to in every market, and the boss is still relying on him for some kind of insight. An outside consultant, who works harder to win the assignment than he will to carry it out?

I put out the question and get back a whole lot of nothing, because the truth is, most of these guys are surrounded at work by yes-men and sycophants who are mostly concerned with keeping their jobs and skimming a little off the top for themselves. So then I ask them about the people they work with in their personal lives, and the answers are completely different. Here they're on top of it. Here they've got the best lawyers, the best accountants, the best architects designing their second homes, the best masseuses, the best doctors . . . Hell, they've probably got the best second-opinions lined up, to make sure the first guy gets it right.

My point is, most successful businessmen and women don't take the same care in their professional lives as they do in their personal lives, and if you mean to succeed in business you've got to make it personal. Nobody would run your business like you, or they'd be your boss. Figure it out, if you've inherited an executive team that can't quite distinguish its butt from its elbow, you need to make some changes. Figure it out, if there's someone outside your company whose insights you've come to respect and admire, you might want to bring that person on board. Figure it out, if your kids are spending your money on this or that new technology or product, in an area that's somewhat related to your own, there are probably some things you should be doing differently to redirect some of that money your way. Come on, it doesn't get more basic than this: your kids are taking your hard-earned money and giving it to somebody who's taking your space in the market. It's not just that you don't understand your kids or what they're into, but you're helping your competitors.

You're giving them that all-important edge—and you're putting it on your own credit card.

Start listening to the people who actually have something to say—and tuning out the chatter that will slow you down and run you right out of business.

I'll close out with a story that illustrates the kind of drive that has fueled our successes in the urban market, the kind you don't often see and can't help but admire. Doesn't matter what industry you're talking about, relentless determination almost always rises to the top, and in this department my boy Puffy has got it. Understand, this particular story happens to be about Puffy, but I can tell similar stories about anybody who's put in the kind of work it takes to make it. Irv Gotti. Fat Joe. Chris Lighty. Steve Stoute. LL Cool J. Russell Simmons. Fabolous. Dr. Dre. Pharrell. Hype Williams. Jamie Foxx. Shakim and Queen Latifah. Ja Rule. Mary J. Blige. Kedar Massenburg. Kevin Lyles. And on and on. Could even be about me and my FUBU partners. You always hear comments about how artists and industry heads run around getting high and shooting each other, but I've met many business tycoons from all different industries and few rival the drive, determination and focus you'll see on this list, and across our market.

Okay, so here's the story: Puffy invited me out to Los Angeles to go to the Oscars. It was 1998, the year *Titanic* won all those awards, and he wanted to talk to me about a clothing line he was thinking about starting up. I was always up for a road trip and an unexpected good time, and I was happy to share some of my insights about the fashion industry. At that time, no artist had been successful starting up his own clothing line, and I told Puffy I didn't think it was a good idea. Wasn't because I didn't want to see him as a competitor, but because I didn't want him to lose his shirt. He was a friend of mine. My thinking was, There's plenty of business to go around. And my experience was, It's a tough market, and the kids have some kind of radar that tells them these rappers don't have the first idea about clothes or fashion or whatever. A lot of artists had put their name on some upstart lines, and nobody seemed to care. The thinking among some of these starch-white fashion companies was to take a black guy with a bald head, put him in their clothes, stamp their logo in his hand, and hope there's some cache by association among the teens and tweens and Generation Y-types who follow this type of thing. But like I said, consumers today are smarter than ever before. They know when they're being jerked around, so they stayed away each time out.

But Puffy said, "Don't worry, D, I'm an artist. I'm fashionable. I was fashionable before I became successful."

I couldn't argue with him on this. There were a few of us on his private jet, and we got the party started at altitude, so we didn't *just* talk about Puffy's clothing line. In fact, we hardly talked about it at all, just touched on it every here and there. When we landed in L.A., we went straight to the Academy Awards ceremony, and then on to a bunch of Oscar night parties, which for me was like a slap in the face. I mean, this was 1998, and FUBU had been popping for a couple years; I was fairly well known, but I got out to Los Angeles, and I was at a party with Leonardo DiCaprio, and Arnold Schwarzenegger, and Clint Eastwood, and I just felt ridiculous. They might as well have given me a tray with some drinks on it, because I was nobody in this crowd.

Nobody, somebody . . . it didn't matter. We went at it hard, all night long. It was me, Puffy, J. Lo, Andre Harrell, Heavy D and my partner Keith. We finally shut it down at about eight in the morning, which on our east coast clock was even later (or, earlier, if you want to look at it that way). I put my head down for a second and started to nod off when Puffy called me and said, "D, let's get ready, we've got to be on the jet at ten."

I thought, What the hell is this guy made of? Really, I was twisted.

We'd been up all night, partying hard, after flying out the day before. We went to the Oscars, and then to all these private Oscar parties, and now we had to hustle on over to the airport. Then we got on the plane and talked for about two hours. Then Puffy laid down in the middle of the floor of the jet, folded his arms across his chest and closed his eyes. He zoned everything out. I sat and fidgeted in my seat, trying to get comfortable, and every once in a while I'd catch Puffy out of the corner of my eye, laying like a dead man on the floor of the cabin, without a care in the world. He slept that way for about two hours.

I'd assumed we were going back to New York, because nobody had indicated otherwise, but about four hours after taking off from L.A. it became clear we were headed to Boston, where Puffy had a show to do. Puffy certainly hadn't let on by his behavior the night before that he had a concert. I might have known. It was the middle of his world tour. We got to Boston, and there was a police escort to meet us at the airport and lead us to the arena. We didn't stop at a hotel to freshen up, didn't stop to get something to eat, just went directly to the stage. Puffy changed on the way over. The place was packed, and people were just going crazy, and he put on a serious, relentless show for the next three hours. His energy level was off the hook, then right after that we were whisked off to some after-party, where he had to do a little meet and greet thing for a couple hours, then after that we went to a recording studio where he'd booked some time to lay down some new tracks. And all during this time, he was on the phone every five minutes, giving interviews, making deals and handling the artists at his record label.

I'm exhausted just writing about this now, all these years later, but Puffy was like a wind-up toy. He just kept going and going, and at the other end I understood what he means when he says, "We won't stop!" That's one of his lines. The guy must have slept maybe two hours in the previous three days—and those were on the floor of the plane! Me, I thought I was gonna die. I was dead, and this guy puts on an incredible show, and then when it's over he's still not done. He bounces up and keeps going. And that's business-as-usual for him. One year, on top of everything else, he even found time to train for the New York Marathon, which I thought was just sick. Incredible, but sick.

Discipline, that's the key. A guy like Puffy, he sees something he wants, and he goes after it hard. Doesn't matter if it's in his personal life, or his professional life, or if it's over some start-up enterprise that seeks to combine the two. He's just one of those relentless, tireless individuals, and it's an inspiring thing to see. *Time* magazine, in naming him one of the most influential people in the world, described Puffy as "a force of nature," but it's not natural, the energy this man has, the focus, the determination. It's something else entirely.

The outcome on Puffy's clothing line was he wanted me to distribute it. At the time, I wasn't ready to take on a whole other line, so I suggested he get in touch with a friend of mine named Jeff Tweedy, who had some experience in this area, and that's how it played out. Jeff ended up heading Sean John for the next six years, and helped to make it a major force in men's fashion. When they launched, Sean John was our only serious competitor. They took a big bite out of us, but it was bound to happen that some other line would emerge and give us a run. There was Puffy's Sean John, and soon after that there was Jay-Z's RocaWear, two artist-based lines that worked in a big way because the artists who were out in front of them were known as fashionable trendsetters. These guys had style.

I share this story because everyone thinks rappers are a bunch of hard-charging party animals, up all night, drinking champagne, whatever, and that's often the case. That's how it was with Puffy, too, back in the day, but he was also disciplined and focused and professional. He was calm in the middle of chaos. He set goals for himself and he went after them. And let me tell you, it was something to see.

Outro
CLOUT

I think back to that opening scene at the start
of this book, the one with my face down on the lawn of my girlfriend's
house on Long Island, a gun to the back of my head, my life flashing
in front of my eyes, me thinking I was about to die, and I recognize
that my story is all about power. But then, everyone's story is about
power, one way or another. What sets us apart is how we play it.

At just that moment on my girlfriend's lawn, the guy with the gun
was in control, but I realize now he didn't have any real power over
me. Yeah, he could have put a bullet in my head and taken my life *and*
my car, but that's not any kind of power. Anyway, that's not *real*
power. That's not the kind of power people write books about. That
was a display of cowardice more than anything else, a bullying tactic
carried out by some low-life with a weapon who would never know
what it meant to be truly in charge, to harness his God-given strengths
and overcome his inevitable weaknesses and lift himself up and out
and beyond his circumstance.

I believe strongly that we're all born with the power to survive and thrive in this world, it's just that some of us haven't figured out how to tap into it. If I've got any kind of message, this is it right here. That guy with the gun, he wouldn't have had the first idea how to use his abilities in any kind of positive way because that's not where his head was at. That little old lady on the strip in Vegas, soft-pedaling the same car as the leadfoot kid in front of her, she couldn't think to look under the hood to discover the power within. Hell, it didn't even occur to her that she *needed* that power. But we've all got the same engine. We've all got the same parts, the same shot at success, or greatness, or accomplishment . . . or whatever it is we're shooting for, and so it's the *display* of that power that separates the *haves* of this world from the *have-nots*. It's the ability to change the way we look out at the world, and the way the world looks back at us. It's identifying that power, and figuring what the hell to do with it. It's knowing to look for it in the first place.

So, yeah, my story is all about power. The FUBU story is all about power. The rise to influence of our hip-hop culture, all about power. When you roll it all up in one big bundle, it's also about decisiveness, agility, dedication, communication, purpose, leadership. It's about the vision to zig when everyone else zags, to see ten steps ahead of you, to react to the fallout before it finds you. It's about surrounding your-self with good people, and finding the best in those people. It's about refusing to give up or take no for an answer. It's about knowing when and how to play your position in the jungle, be it lion or hyena.

I've tried in these pages to be honest and objective about my role in FUBU's launch, and FUBU's place in the hip-hop culture and the culture at large. But everything that's gone down in my life—for us, by us—has come from strength. Power. It comes from the power of my mother, setting all those positive examples. It comes from the power of seeing my boys from the neighborhood heading down all kinds of wrong roads, and knowing there had to be a better path. For me. I'm not saying there's one path we're all meant to follow, but I sure as hell didn't want to wind up dead, or in jail, or stuck in some dead-end job helping someone else pursue his dreams. It comes from the power of getting with strong individuals like my original partners, Keith Perrin, J Alexander and Carl Brown, who recognized an opportunity and were willing to put everything they had into it. It comes from the power of my new partners, Bruce and Norman Weisfeld, who had the courage and power to reach out to four young black guys from the 'hood and trust them to grow their business. It comes from the power of our corporate distributors at Samsung, who had the strength of vision to buy into our vision, our employees at FUBU who helped us to realize that vision, and our core customers, who bought into our line in such a big, determined way we had no choice but to succeed. And it comes from the power of a corporate culture that seems to want to make room for the African-American community in its business plan, even as their traditional models suggest we don't spend money in any kind of meaningful way.

So you see, there's power at every turn. The power could be internal. For example, it wasn't the easiest thing in the world for me to cop to, me wanting to be a designer. I mean, when I was a kid, where I grew up, designers were typically gay, flamboyant and white. For a young black male heterosexual from Hollis to put it out that I wanted to sew hats for a living, and after that to make it as a fashion designer . . . that was tough. I was just begging to be a punching bag around my neighborhood. It took a certain fortitude, I don't mind saying. But I knew who I was and what I wanted, and no amount of peer pressure could have stopped me from pursuing my goal.

Mostly, though, the power is all around. It's under my hood, it's under my partners' hoods, it's under my competitors' hoods, it's under your hood, and it's under the hood of the guy in the car next to you at the stop light. Like I said, we've all got the same engines. Even that low-life who jacked my car all those years ago. Matter of fact, there's a footnote to that Rockville Center hold-up, and it's worth repeating here for the way it shows how power can turn. After this guy made off with my car, after my head cleared a little bit, I tried to puzzle things together, and I had my suspicions about who was involved. I figured it out that there was some guy I knew, some guy who spotted me in that gas station, who then sent one of his boys to follow me and jack my car. He didn't mean me any physical harm, despite the gun to the back of my head and the throwing me to the ground. He just wanted the car, and whatever cash he could take, because he knew the car was probably insured and the money was probably meaningless to me. It was the way of the street. But he also knew that he couldn't do it himself, because it would come back to bite him, so he sent someone from another one of his crews, one of his stoolies, someone I wouldn't recognize.

And guess what? This guy from the gas station continued to run with the same crowd, the same group of people I used to know from when we were flipping those cars. After a while, he started to talk. I don't know if he was bragging about what he and his boy did to me that night, or if he was looking for some kind of absolution, but he kept running his mouth. He even went to my boy Hype Williams several years later and told him the whole story, and I think Hype must have encouraged him to talk to me because not long after that I got a call from this guy. He'd been in prison. He'd been in and out of all kinds of trouble. Nothing had gone right for this guy, and there he was on the other end of my phone, spinning his story. He said, "D, my life ain't right. It's never been right since then."

I said, "So why you on the phone with me? You think I've put some curse on you?"

The guy was kind of fumbling on the other end of the phone, like he didn't know what to say, so I kept talking. "I don't have a beef with you," I said. "What's past is past. I have kids. I'm happy with my life. You still have that street mentality, but I've moved on."

He said, "So we cool? We straight?"

Soon as he said it I thought, It's a funny thing, power. One moment this guy's got it behind the prop of a gun. His stoolie was in control, so he was in control by extension, but then the next moment it bounces back to me. Might have taken a couple years for that next moment to roll around, but it always rolls around, and when it finally did the power had shifted. Big time. To where this guy was desperate and pathetic and pretty much begging me to let him off the hook for what he'd done. And I did. I cut him loose, told him we were straight. And I guess we were, because I realized, This guy can't touch me. Truth was, I hadn't thought about this guy in years. He was nothing to me. Hadn't thought about that hold-up in Rockville Center, either. It's like I forgot it had ever happened. But I was thinking about it now that he had called. Put my head right back in that moment. And I realized, this low-life could get one of his boys to stick a gun to the back of my head, but I would always have the upper hand because I knew how to tap that engine I had racing under my hood. I knew to look for that power within, and I knew how to put it to use. We might have started out at the same place, but I'd stepped on the gas and passed this guy by a long time ago.

Acknowledgments
HELP

THROUGHOUT MY LIFE, I HAVE MET THE FULL GAMUT OF BILLIONAIRES, MURDERERS, ACTIVISTS, ICONS, DEVILS, ANGELS, LEADERS, FOLLOWERS, PRIESTS AND PIMPS. THEY ALL HAD ONE THING IN COMMON—SOMETHING THEY HAD, SOMETHING THEY LOST, OR SOMETHING THEY WANTED. AND THAT SOMETHING WAS POWER. I'VE TRIED TO TAKE THAT AWAY FROM EACH ENCOUNTER, EVEN WHEN THINGS DIDN'T GO MY WAY, BECAUSE IF I'VE LEARNED ONE THING IN THIS LIFE IT'S THIS: EVEN IF YOU LOSE, DON'T LOSE THE LESSON.

NEEDLESS TO SAY, I HAVE LEARNED A LOT OF LESSONS. I ONLY EXIST BECAUSE OF ALL THE PEOPLE WHO HAVE LAID THE GROUNDWORK FOR ME TO WALK IN MOST DOORS AND KICK IN SOME OTHERS, FROM MARTIN LUTHER KING, MALCOLM X, MUHAMMAD ALI, RICHARD PRYOR AND NAT KING COLE, TO ALL THE ENTREPRENEURS, ARTISTS AND EVERYDAY PEOPLE WHO HAVE INSPIRED ME. I HAVE A FULL UNDERSTANDING THAT I STAND ON THE SHOULDERS OF GIANTS, AND I REALIZE I WOULD NOT BE IN A POSITION TO SHARE MY EXPERIENCES IN THIS BOOK WERE IT NOT FOR THE COUNTLESS OTHERS WHO HAVE GONE BEFORE ME.

AND SO TO THESE FINAL NOTES . . . I CAN'T PLAY AN INSTRUMENT AND I CAN BARELY HOLD A NOTE IN THE BATHTUB, SO THESE WORDS WILL BE THE CLOSEST I'LL GET TO WRITING THE THANK YOU MESSAGES YOU SEE ON THE BACKS OF ALBUM COVERS. I LOVE TO READ THOSE LINER NOTES, AND I SHARE MY OWN VERSION HERE. THIS IS A NOD TO ALL THE PEOPLE WHO HAVE PLAYED A ROLE IN MY LIFE, PEOPLE WHO HAVE HELPED ME OR INFLUENCED ME OR CHALLENGED ME TO DO BETTER. THERE ARE MANY PEOPLE I MIGHT HAVE LEFT OFF OF THESE SHOUT-OUTS . . . PLEASE FORGIVE ME . . . I'M SURE YOU WILL TELL ME ABOUT IT . . . HERE GOES . . .

THIS IS TO CARL, KEITH AND J . . . THANK YOU FOR THE BROTHERHOOD

THIS IS TO MY GRANDMOTHER, VIOLA COPPEDGE, AND MY GRANDFATHER, ARTHUR COPPEDGE . . . I KNOW THEY'RE BOTH SMILING DOWN ON ME WITH PRIDE

THIS IS TO THE WEISFELD FAMILY . . . THANK YOU FOR THE TRUST.

THIS IS TO LESLIE SHORT . . . YOU ARE THE BEST AND HAVE ALWAYS HAD MY BACK. JOE LEVIN . . . SELL SELL SELL. GRIM . . . THERE COULD NEVER BE ENOUGH THANKS FOR GUARDING MY LIFE. FIX YA FACE. MAL . . . 'YA FRIED BUT I LOVE 'YA. THE DRIVER . . . THEY LOVE ME FOR YOU. SIMONE . . . YOU ARE THE GREATEST. OLEG. PIVEN. STUFFY! LARRY BLENDEN . . . SHARP AS A RAZOR AND BALLS OF STEEL. JARED . . . SMART, YOUNG AND GOOD-LOOKING! DON'T GET GASSED. KYLIE . . . YOU ARE THE SMARTEST PERSON I KNOW. TUTT . . . ALL THE WAY FROM RED LOBSTER, BABY! WHAT! OMAR RODRIGUEZ . . . MY MAN. TREVOR CLARK . . . MY WINGMAN. CHAMP . . . THE VOICE OF REASON. BLACKERRR AND BIG PAT, THE FUBU RYDERS. BOBBY JOSEPH . . . THE HOTTEST DESIGNER IN THE GAME, HANDS DOWN. BARRY BLUE . . . IF I WASN'T ME, I'D WANT TO BE YOU. COPEN . . . A GENIUS AND MY FRIEND. RAJ . . . PLS SHIP ON TIME. DAVID HOROWITZ. EDNA. CORENA, MAYBELL AND CHRIS . . . MY PICKERS. ALI. RACHAEL. BLESS BERNARDO . . . HER NAME SAYS IT ALL. ERMY.

VAL. KIKI PETERSON . . . YOU WERE ALWAYS THERE FOR ME, THANKS. TIE. PRIMO. TYSON . . . SPRINKLING THE STONES. BIG KEITH . . . LV. MIMI. GORILLA FORCE. JOE AND RALPH NAKASH. EDDIE FROM JORDACHE. JULIAN FROM FRANCE. BABBS FROM GERMANY. SUKI LEE . . . THANK YOU FOR THE MANY YEARS OF SUPPORT. TONY LACANTE . . . A GREAT BUSINESS MAN. RONNIE AND PEERLESS. LARU. STEVE ARNOLD. DANNY AND RADU . . . THANKS FOR COMING AND HELPING US STEP UP OUR GAME. CHARLIE. MR. CHO . . . YOU ARE THE MAN. THERESA . . . YOU CONTROL THE MONEY, SO I GUESS I SHOULD CALL YOU THE BOSS. I'M GRATEFUL THAT YOU'RE ON MY SIDE.

KEITH CLINKSCALE . . . THE MEANING OF CLASS. RAY AND LOUIS FROM BET . . . STRONG ,SMART AND BLACK. MARTY FROM BET. SANDRA STERN . . . THE MEANING OF COOL. LARRY MILLER . . . THE BRAINS OF BRAND JORDAN. BERNIE YUMAN . . . SAY, SAY, SAY. PLS SHOW ME MORE POWER! BOX AL HAS-SAS AND RIZA IZAD . . . THANK YOU FOR BELIEVING IN ME TO GET THIS BOOK DONE. COWBOY, MJ LATIMER, KEDAR. LL . . . I'M STILL YA BIGGEST FAN, HOMIE! DARRYL MILLER . . . BRILLIANT LEGAL MIND. JAMES D . . . I'M WAIT-ING ON YOU PIMPIN'. HYPE WILLIAMS . . . THE MAD SCIENTIST. CHRIS ROBINSON, JESSY TERRERO, DR. TEETH, ERICK WHITE, OMARI, PONCH, DER-RICK, MALIKE . . . THE GENIUSES. BARRY GORDON AT IMAGE. CHARLES KLEIN, BILL COX, RICH WAGER AND FAMILY. LOU, HARD EARN, CONRAD QUARLES, MACHO, GENE NUSBAUM AND FAMILY. CHRISTIAN BIKOWSKI. CURT, ROBERT KIM, DEBRA GRABIAN. JOANNA . . . YOU ARE THE BEST. THANKS FOR BEING ON MY SIDE. IO, FILIP ICON ENT. PHIL MACK, DRE THE EDITOR, NOMI, HEATHER, RONNIE THE JEWELER, BIG MIKE, SNAGS. RICHARD PILSON. STEVE AND DEBBIE, BILL STEPHANIE AND MOM . . . THANKS FOR TAKING CARE OF MY BABIES. BIG TIM IN THE HOUSE! GENE RIGGINS, BURNT PHAT FARM, WAYNE, FLA. ED WOODS, LONDEL, JAMES. TONY RASHAAN. BIG SHORTY, JEROME, KATE SOUTHERLAND, CHAKA AND JEFF, LYNN BERNETT, KENARD GIBBS, MARVETT BRITTO . . . KEEP KILLIN 'EM, GIRL. RON GUTTA, JIMMY HENCHMAN, AL MONDAY . . . SEE 'YA SOON. CAT, RA RIGHT RIGHTS. BOB, ANDREA AND GARY . . . YOU GUYS HELPED ME

FROM DAY ONE. BERNARD CAHN . . . R.I.P. HENRY COPPEDGE . . . THANKS, UNC. R.I.P. ANTONIO, CLUB BED. HERMAN FROM DUB MAGAZINE . . . LET'S GET THIS MONEY. REY . . . YOU WILL ALWAYS HAVE MY BACK AND I LOVE YOU FOR IT. MIKE DYSON . . . ENLIGHTEN ME, BABY. REECE AND DAYMOND . . . GEORGE FRAZER SPEAK TO 'EM. SMAC ENT. TOMMY POOCH, GEORGE AND REGINA DANIALS . . . POPS! HOW DO YOU DO IT! R KELLY. REV. FLOYD FLAKE . . . THE MOST INFLUENTIAL AND DYNAMIC SPEAKER I HAVE EVER HAD THE HONOR OF MEETING. THANK YOU FOR ALL THE ADVICE! LORI TROTTER . . . THANK YOU FOR ALWAYS BEING THERE FOR ME.

DAN PAISNER . . . YOU MADE THIS BOOK EASY. YOU ALSO TAUGHT ME SOME VERY VALUABLE THINGS ABOUT MYSELF. YOU WERE DAMN NEAR MY SHRINK. THANK YOU.

DAN STRONE OF TRIDENT MEDIA GROUP . . . YOU GOT THIS DEAL GOING.

REBEKAH AND STAFF AT NAKED INK . . . GREAT PEOPLE, FOCUSED PEOPLE AND PROFESSIONALS. LET'S HAVE FUN WITH THIS!

TO ALL THE CONSUMERS WHO HAVE SUPPORTED ME FOR YEARS . . . YOU SPENT YOUR HARD-EARNED MONEY ON MY DESIGNS, IDEAS AND DREAMS AND THEN WORE THEM ON YOUR BODIES AND DRESSED THE ONES YOU LOVE IN THEM. THAT'S HUGE. THANK YOU FOR BELIEVING.

LINX, TIGGA, JASON, JUSTIN TIMBERLAKE, JESSE JACKSON, IRV GOTTI, CHRIS GOTTI . . . NOW THAT 'YA BACK, DON'T HURT 'EM TOO HARD! MARK WAHLBERG AND JAMAL. JA RULE . . . HIT ME WITH THE HEAT, HOMIE. PUFFY, MARY J. BLIGE AND KENDU . . . CLASS ACTS. DJ IREA . . . YOU ARE INCREDIBLE. BEING YOUR MANAGER IS AN HONOR! WYCLEFF AND BEAST, LENOX LEWIS THE UNDIS-PUTED, PRINCE THE ARTIST . . . THANKS FOR MAKING MY DREAMS COME TRUE. MONTEL WILLIAMS . . . LET'S HIT THE SLOPES, BABY! CHRIS BROWN AND FAMILY. LUDACRIS . . . ONE OF THE SLICKEST LYRICISTS IN THE GAME.

MRS. JONES . . . YOU GAVE ME ONE OF MY FIRST BREAKS. BRAND NUBIAN, JERMAINE DUPRI . . . YOU INSPIRE ME, HOMIE. BUSTA . . . STOP CALLING ME FAT WHEN YOU SEE ME.

RECE AND LITTLE DAYMOND . . . MICHAEL MADD . . . CHRIS LIGHTY AND MONA SCOTT . . . PIMPING THE GAME FOR YEARS. I LOVE IT. BUN B, PIMP C, AND RED . . . THREE MEN OF HONOR. SLIM THUG AND FAMILY . . . REAL PEOPLE. ERICK NICKS . . . A&R ROYALTY. FABULOUS CHAO AND CAMP . . . LET'S GET IT. KELLY G AND STEVEN HILL . . . THE GATEKEEPERS, STYLISTS WHO HAVE KEPT US HOT FOREVER. JUNE AMBROS . . . KNOCK 'EM DEAD WITH THE BOOK, BABY. TERRELL, ROGER, MONICA, MIA AND MANY, MANY MORE.

RUSSEL SIMMONS . . . EVERYBODY'S SILENT PARTNER AND ONE OF THE FIRST MEN I EVER WITNESSED AS A YOUNG BOY IN HOLLIS DOING IT BIG AND SHOW-ING ME THERE WERE OTHER ROUTES TO SUCCESS.

STEVEN COLVIN . . . MAXIM IS STILL THE SEXIEST BOOK OUT. DON FRANCA-CHINI . . . FOR YOU TO CALL ME THE CALVIN KLEIN OF OUR GENERATION WAS THE BIGGEST HONOR OF ALL. DENISE RICH . . . THE ESSENCE PARTY WAS A BLAST, THANK YOU. DAVID WINTERS . . . I'M READY WHEN YOU ARE. PETER ARNELL . . . YOU AND BERNIE EQUAL POWER. HERMAN DUB MAGAZINE . . . LET'S GET FOCUSED, BABY. CAROLYN BYRD . . . TO BE ANYWHERE NEAR YOUR LEVEL IS A DREAM. DENNIS PUBLISHING . . . YOU SECRETLY OWN THE MAR-KET. MARK ECKO AND SETH . . . SHOW 'EM HOW TO DO IT.

PATTY WEBSTER . . . BELYA DINA . . . BETH AND LYNE BURNET FROM VIBE . . . EGYPT . . . STEVE HARVEY . . . TALENT . . . GEORGE FRAPHER, MICHAEL DYSON . . . MIKE JOHN OF URBAN WIRELESS . . . DAYE MAYS . . . STAR AND BUCK WILD . . . CHAD . . . SARAH RAINMAKER . . . BELVIANNA TODMANN.

TRAV AND RICHIE . . . . IT'S ABOUT TO POP! WILLIE ESCO, DJ CLUE, D NICE MOGUL, SPACE BABY, S&S, KID CAPRI, BIZZ, LS1, MAURICIO, KHALID, FRANKIE

NEEDLES, GEORGE DUKES, CHRIS AND ROMAN JONES . . . YOU HAVE THE HOTTEST CLUBS IN THE COUNTRY AND IT'S ONLY 'CAUSE YOU CATS ARE HOT! KEEP DOING 'YA THINGS. PIMPS BENNY BOOM, WEKEEM, RUFF RYDERS, SHAKA AND QUEEN LATIFAH, SHERYL LEE RALPH, ZABB JUDAH, FLOYD MAY-WEATHER, LORENZ TATE, WINKIE WRIGHT, ED LOVE, RICK ROSS, E CLASS, STAR AND BUCK WILD . . . I'M WAITING TO HEAR YOU BACK OUT THERE, BABY. MAGIC JOHNSON . . . THE BEST. SPIKE LEE . . . THANKS FOR THE PRIVATE JET RIDES TO THE GAMES. BILL SPECTOR, TYSON BECKFORD, PATTY LABELLE, PHARELL AND ROB, SCOTT STORCH AND DERRICK, STEVE STOUT . . . YOU TRICKED THEM AT THEIR OWN GAME AND I LOVE IT. TAVIS SMILEY, JOHN SINGLETON, TYREES AND DUQUAN. JAMIE FOSTER BROWN . . . GREAT LADY. URBAN WORLD WIRE-LESS, MIKE JOHN, DATWON, INDUSTRY INSIDER, FEDS ANTONIO, DON DIVA VIBE. THANK YOU, THANK YOU, THANK YOU.

Special Thanks To:

FUBU THE COLLECTION

COOGI

CROWN HOLDER COLLECTION

S T E A L T H

[branding corp]

MOGULSONLY

CHECK OUT THESE ADDITIONAL TITLES

The official guide to the "Hot Mom" movement

ISBN: 1-5955-5851-9

A moving photographic tribute to the survivors of Hurricane Katrina

ISBN: 1-5955-5857-8

The dramatic adventures and accomplishments of Skip Yowell and one of the world's most recognized brands

ISBN: 1-5955-5852-7

For more information about Naked Ink books, online newsletters, and exclusive offers, visit us at www.nakedink.net.